PRIVATE AND CONFIDENTIAL.

SENSATIONAL RELIGION;

AS RESORTED TO IN THE SYSTEM CALLED THE
"SALVATION ARMY,"

IN ITS INFLUENCE UPON THE YOUNG

AND

IN ITS EFFECT UPON THE DUTIES AND CLAIMS
OF HOME LIFE.

BY THE

REV. SAMUEL CHARLESWORTH,
Formerly Rector of Limpsfield, Surrey, and of Limehouse, East London.

Printed only for circulation privately among the relatives and friends
of Mr Charlesworth's family.

PREFACE.

THREE years since I had in my home a dear daughter, my youngest child, then aged sixteen years, who was a most loving, dutiful, and truthful girl; the joy and cheer of my home life, as an affectionate companion and a sympathising helper in my parochial work in the schools and among the poor.

That child is now entirely alienated from me and her relatives and former friends; she has deserted her home, forsaken the Church of her youth, of which she was a confirmed member and a communicant. She has, against my wish and earnest remonstrance, made her home in the house of Mr William Booth, to one of whose sons she has engaged herself to be married, without my consent, though now only nineteen years of age. She has given herself up to the Army service for life, and told me that the orders of her "General" are more binding upon her than my wishes and directions. This harmful influence exerted by Mr Booth and his family over my poor misguided child has been obtained in opposition to my most strenuous exertions, and in defiance of my earnest remonstrances and entreaties. All that I, as a loving devoted father could do to rescue my child from what I felt to be a most demoralising influence, I have attempted.

PREFACE.

The painful narrative in this pamphlet is a detail of some, but only a small portion of those efforts. Fain would I be silent, but I feel that it is due to my position as a clergyman and a Christian parent, to explain to my relatives and friends and to justify the course which I have already taken, and may hereafter be compelled to take, with reference to my daughter's connection with the army and Mr Booth's family.

SAMUEL CHARLESWORTH.

IPSWICH, *June* 1885.

SENSATIONAL RELIGION.

CHAPTER I.

In the year 1870, when I became Rector of Limehouse, there was, in the parish, a branch of an Evangelization Society, called the "Christian Mission," which had recently been organised by the Rev. Wm. Booth in East London, the head-quarters of the Mission then being in Whitechapel. The Limehouse branch occupied a room opposite the parish church. The mission workers were earnest, devoted men; the members were drawn principally from the artisan and labouring classes, engaged in shipbuilding and in the docks. Several of them became members of a large Sunday Bible-class held by my dear wife, and united in her weekly prayer meetings. She found them simple-minded, true-hearted Christian men of consistent life and conduct. The mission work was carried on by street-preaching and short services, followed up by after meetings in the Mission room. It appeared to us both to be a very useful blessed work, and it had our warmest sympathy and cordial co-operation. The magistrates of the Thames Police Court having forbidden the street services to be held on a small vacant piece of ground opposite to the rectory house, I gladly allowed the use of my front garden court, opening on to the main road, with wide carriage gates, for these services. For several years the Mission workers met there on Sunday afternoon until the prohibition by the magistrates was withdrawn, so that the services could be again held in the streets of the parish.

During the twelve years of my incumbency of Limehouse I never met any member of Mr Booth's family in the parish, and I had no knowledge whatever of him or them, excepting that one day he came in to my church vestry to ask if I would lend to his workers one of my school-rooms in which to hold services. After the Christian Mission had been thus carrying on its successful work among the poor of East London for eight or ten years, Mr Booth decided upon adopting a modification in the character of the mission by changing it into the organisation and system called the "Salvation Army." To my regret I afterwards observed what appeared to me to be a great deterioration in the character of the mission. Flags waved over the entrance of the mission-room. Immense placards covered the front of the building, setting forth the military titles of the various officers, male and female, who would conduct the services, making prominent allusion to the formerly abandoned lives of some so selected; the subjects of the addresses were described in language which I often shuddered to read, the person, name, and work of the Lord Jesus Christ and of the Holy Spirit being, as it seemed to me, so irreverently alluded to, and mixed up with things so incongruous to holy and reverential feelings. The building being in a main road leading from the city to the East and West India Docks, ships' officers, and sailors of all nations were constantly noticing these placards. As each day I had frequent occasion to pass and repass, I used to overhear the coarse comments which these announcements called forth from them. The street processions were now of a very noisy character. On Sunday they were led so close past our church at morning and evening service as materially to disturb the congregation; also preliminary open-air services used to be held at the corner of a street, leading to the principal entrance of the church, so blocking up the path, that I and my family and many others going to church had to pass round another way. Many remonstrances were made to me by the church officers and members of the congregation on these annoyances; so at length I wrote to Mr Booth in a kind tone and friendly spirit, expressing my great regret at the change he had made in the character of his mission and its work. In reply he stated that the alteration was the result of much consideration, and that he had no reason to question its desirableness and utility. So things went on until after the death of my wife, in November 1881, when my failing health and strength compelled me to resign a parish, the work of which was so arduous and anxious.

CHAPTER II.

IT is now my painful task to narrate how my child was brought under the influence of Mr Booth and his family, rendered the more sorrowful and painful, because the memory of my dear wife is connected with it ; and her letters, and my own letters have to be made public, as the only means of supporting my statements and refuting the mis-statements of others.

The members of my wife's Bible-class who belonged to the Salvation Army continued faithful in their adhesion to her. In consequence of her knowing many men and women who had joined the Army, both in her classes and in her mother's meetings, my wife's interest was strongly drawn forth towards this new phase of mission work. Occasionally she went into the hall opposite to the church in our parish, and would take friends visiting us, and our children with her. She also attended some of the holiness meetings in the Whitechapel Mission Room and in Exeter Hall. Though thus in her large heartedness and Christian love she shewed her full sympathy in the work, she entirely agreed with me on the subject of those features in it which I considered objectionable. But her naturally enthusiastic temperament was in accord with the intense earnestness and sensational appeals of these meetings.

In the summer of 1881 my wife's health began to fail. Twelve years of incessant labour among the poor of Limehouse, in crowded factories, hot mission rooms, and close cottages, added to constant exposure late at night, to the foggy and cold atmosphere of a riverside parish, wore out a frame not constitutionally robust, whilst an insidious internal disease unknown to her and her family was also undermining her strength and working death. Nobly and unwaveringly she toiled on in her labours of love, not only in the parish but in many other calls elsewhere, to serve her loved Lord and Master. At length the death of her aged beloved father, in the month of September of that year, gave a shock to the frail frame, from which she could not rally; and in the month of November following she fell asleep in Jesus peacefully, calmly, and rejoicingly in the beloved home of her childhood on Clapham Common.

Here I must refer in connection with her memory to statements which have been made, that she thrust our child Maud on the Booth family; that it was her wish that Maud should unite herself to the Army for life as an officer; and even that it had been her dying desire that she should marry one of Mr Booth's sons, on which pretence he came to me and claimed her hand in marriage. All these statements, made after her death, when her own lips could not refute them, are mere inventions, utterly untrue. I was by her bedside, with my three children, the whole of the last week of her life. I took down in writing her dying wishes with reference to them. Not one word was ever said, not one thought expressed, justifying any of these assertions; on the contrary, I have many letters written during the last six months of her life, showing that no such wishes could ever have entered her thoughts. The separation of her child from her father, her sisters, and the home and Church of her youth, demanded by the Army Service Regulations, would have been abhorrent to so loving and devoted a wife and mother.

I refer to these cruel allegations because they have been made public in newspaper letters and platform addresses. My relatives and friends will well understand how deeply it must wound my feelings and those of my other loving and dutiful children to allude to such a subject. But the memory of my wife is too dear and sacred to me not to shield it from the imputation that she would, unknown to me, have encouraged my child to desert me and her home, and to harbour the thought of marriage to any one when she was a girl at school only sixteen years of age. To all who knew her and revere her loved memory, these inventions will be palpably false; but as many, who are strangers to me and mine, have unhappily formed their opinion of the conduct of the Booth family and of my poor misguided child influenced by these statements, I must insert here extracts from two of her letters out of many to a similar effect. It is intensely painful to me thus to bring to light portions of letters from my wife to my child, but let those who have made these statements to justify their heartless conduct bear the odium of thus harrowing the feelings of a husband and a father almost beyond endurance by this cruel necessity.

EXTRACT from a Letter written by my wife to my child, then at school, about three months before her death.

"LIMEHOUSE RECTORY, *July* 25*th*, 1881.

"My Dear Child,—Do not come home too full of the Booths and the Army. I do so hope you will try to keep your mind from being taken up with this one subject, and try to throw your heart into our own work, where I trust you will help me. I shall be so glad of your help this week, but if you are only thinking of the Army, other sober work will seem dull to you. I have not called on Mrs Booth, and I do not think we are likely to know any of the Booths. It will be very delightful to have you home."

EXTRACT from a Letter from my wife to my child, who had returned to school again, written only five weeks before her death.

"CLAPHAM COMMON, S.W., *October* 1, 1881.

"Now my own Maudie, put all this nonsense about the Booths out of your poor little head; it will do you *great harm* if it goes on. It will dishonour Christ, give you a low double motive, prevent your eye being single (see what Christ says about this in St Matthew); it will also make your poor sick mother *very anxious*, and prevent your being the comfort you might be. Your ever loving mother, "M. A. CHARLESWORTH."

I could add many other extracts, showing how my wife would have recoiled from sanctioning her child in taking the step which so shortly after her death the Booths induced her to take, by alienating her from me, her sisters, and her home, as I shall afterwards shew. May these extracts suffice to free the memory of my wife from the shadow of a suspicion that she would, unknown to me, have counselled my child to unite herself to the Army or to engage herself to be married to a man whose photograph, in this last letter, she forbid her to have, because he was unknown to her as a friend —known only as an Army officer.

I would, before I close this chapter, add a few words in explanation of the conduct of my beloved child, once so loving and devoted to me. How was it that the Booth family could allure her away from me and our home into their system, and entirely alienate her from her relatives and former friends and the Church of her youth? I can in part explain the how and why.

She loved her mother with the most ardent affection. Shortly after her mother's death she returned to school. I can realize the aching void in that susceptible heart, the terrible blank in that youthful life. She had been led by that mother to take a warm interest in the work of the Army; she had been at one of the meetings casually introduced to one of Mr Booth's daughters, with whom she afterwards commenced a correspondence. Moreover, one of the sons, who at the after meetings, spoke to her about her spiritual state, and while so doing held her hand in his, as he acknowledged to me, had thus called forth strong feelings of interest towards him. Her natural temperament was excitable, enthusiastic, and very impulsive; she was then only sixteen years of age. On her return to school she had, in the overwhelming sorrow of her first great grief, sought comfort in writing to that member of the Booth family with whom she had been permitted to hold a correspondence; and through the communications thus held with her, Maud became persuaded that the Army meetings had been productive in her of conversion, and that she was specially called by the Lord to enter his service by joining the Army. Then came in also the human natural element to strengthen this conviction; her admiration for her spiritual adviser, a colonel in the army, on the field staff of the General Commander-in-Chief. Many were the letters passing between that grief-stricken child and her newly adopted friend; she had been fascinated with the excitement and enthusiasm of the great Army meetings in Exeter Hall, her young affections were drawn forth towards her kind and sympathising spiritual adviser and his ardent sister. Oh! I can, as a father, read the secret history of that dear child in her great sorrow as she turned to those comforters; they too could read it, and avail themselves of it. One, so sweet in person, so intelligent and enthusiastic, with wealth in prospect, would be a gain both to the Army and to the family. Thus I lost my child. The twofold cord of religious feeling and love attachment so closely woven into her young life, so tightly drawn around her, was sufficient to allure her from the once loved home, and her father and sisters, and former church associations; it helped to fill up that great void, to supply in part the terrible blank. I can understand it all, and see why and how she deserted me and her home, when such materials were so deftly woven into the woof of her inexperienced young life and character. The religious feeling alone would not have drawn her from me; but the combination with it of the heart attachment did so effectually and completely, more especially when she afterwards found that I disapproved of so early an engagement and of so premature a marriage.

CHAPTER III.

IN the last chapter I have been obliged, not only to anticipate events somewhat, but to refer to circumstances of which I had no knowledge until long after my wife's death.

My child returned to school in the country by her own choice, and I resumed for a time my arduous duties at Limehouse. I was then entirely ignorant of the influence the Army system had exerted over her, and of her acquaintance with any of the Booth family. I knew that she had been with her mother to some meetings of the Army, and that both of them sympathised in the movement; but I never dreamed of her thinking of joining the Army, or of her being engaged to any member of the Booth family, all of whom were entire strangers to me personally. At the Christmas holidays she returned home to me. Then for the first time I ascertained how strong a hold the Army had won upon her interest. She had most of Mrs Booth's publications; she weekly received by post the *War Cry*, and, I have reason to believe, often heard from some members of the Booth family; but as it had been my rule to let my children, after the age of fifteen years, correspond freely with friends, I never saw her letters written to them or those written to her. Finding how intense her feeling was toward the Army, I determined to ascertain something about the movement from my own observations, that I might judge how far it was well for her to be further associated with it. I read and talked over with her several of Mrs Booth's books, and I went with her to three or four meetings.

The result produced on my mind was, that Mrs

Booth's books were very practical, useful expositions of Christian truth and doctrine, most forcibly and clearly explained and applied; but the Army meetings seemed to me to be far too exciting, in an unhealthy unnatural form, for a child of her impulsive, enthusiastic temperament; moreover, the expositions of Scripture there, seemed to me to give a strained perverted view of Christian doctrine. Conversion was regarded as the immediate effect of coming up to the penitent form and making there a confession of sin; holiness of heart and life was considered to be an inevitable consequence which followed. The hymns, addresses, prayers, and the testimonies of experience all led up to a culminating point of excitement, the mental crisis of which was a moral forcing of the aroused to go up to the penitent form, where confession of sin would be followed by an immediate assurance of pardon, and the gift of eternal life with its accompaniment of perfect holiness. On one occasion my child asked leave to go and sit by her friend, Miss Emma Booth, who presided over the penitent form. To my surprise, in the course of the evening she rose with many others to bear her testimony to her conversion, through the Army instrumentality. She spoke earnestly and sweetly, evidently causing an impression throughout the meeting. Long afterwards I learned that when directed by her friend to stand up and give her testimony, she hesitated, saying that I was present, and she did not know if I should like her to do so. She was authoritatively told that she was not to regard what I liked, but what it was her duty to do, in bearing her testimony to the Lord's work in her.

After some weeks spent partly at home and partly with a married sister, she returned to school, leaving on my mind the impression that her spiritual life had not grown in strength or experimental knowledge, but had been morbidly excited, and superficially expanded, and that altogether her state of health, both as to body and mind, was a cause of much anxiety, calling for very watchful supervision and judicious treatment. I wrote strongly on the subject to the friend under whose tuition she was placed, and I looked forward with anxious solicitude to the Easter recess. In the meantime her correspondence went on with her Army friends, and the *War Cry*, a paper then unknown to me, was still her great mental feast week by week.

Towards the close of the school term, and during the Easter recess and the following term, several invitations were written to her to visit the Booths at their house at Clapton; one proposing that she should even go away from school shortly after she had returned to it, in order to attend some Army festive gathering. These invitations were not sent through me, but direct to her in the first instance, so that I had the pain of refusing her earnest request that I would allow her to accept them. Thus the first shadow of a cloud came between an affectionate child and a devoted father, through the persistent sending to her of these successive invitations, after I had decisively refused each previous one. I, at this time, knew nothing of the family; she also had never entered their house, or seen any one of them, excepting at the Army religious meetings. The following is an extract from a letter which I wrote to Miss Emma Booth in reply to the first invitation for Maud to go and visit them:—

"*15th March* 1882.

"As I have thus occasion to write to you, may I add in confidence how intensely anxious I have been about my dear child since her association with the Salvation Army movement. It has produced in her a degree of unnatural morbid excitement which has made me tremble both for body and mind; she is so altered. I would as her father earnestly ask you to moderate, if possible, the extreme exuberance of her feelings. I would not indeed repress one holy thought or desire which may be the result of the Holy Spirit's work, but I feel that at her age, and with her keen sensibilities, a continuance of such religious excitement may be productive of serious mischief, especially as she has lost the guiding controlling influence of her beloved mother. I feel, in my anxiety, inadequate to express in writing my fears or wishes on the subject; perhaps I can best embody what I desire to say in the Apostle Paul's words, 'Let your moderation be known unto all men.'"

I find that my next letter refusing another invitation reiterates, most strongly but more at length, my fears about the injurious effect of the excitement to which my child was being subjected. After giving a special reason why I dreaded sensational meetings or services for her, I added:—

"*27th April* 1882.

"To some sensitive, impulsive, and highly-strung natures like my dear child's, I incline to think and fear that an atmosphere of so much unavoidable excitement and intense strain may prove injurious. At the age of twenty the risk would be far less, but sixteen and seventeen is so critical a period in the development of the mind and character. I have attended three of your meetings with my dear child to watch over the effect. She has wonderful self-command and self-possession, but I can perceive the great strain produced upon her. Her appetite is affected, her whole being is absorbed and concentrated upon the one object. Where conversion is needed and self-consecration is demanded, it is well that such a power, such a force should be brought to bear; but where union to the Lord Jesus, by His Spirit, has been so manifestly wrought, and where unreserved devotion of the heart and life has followed, it seems to me that with such a temperament as hers, at her age, a more tranquil restful atmosphere is desirable. She needs now building up and strengthening. I feel what wisdom and grace it requires in watching over my dear child, on the one hand, not to repress the work of the Spirit of Holiness, but on the other, to bear in mind that the mind and body when not fully developed require gentle, careful training. May God give me grace so to watch over my dear child, that His will with reference to her may be fully accomplished."

Again, a further invitation sent to my child at school called forth another remonstrance from me, which I insert, because it is needful to show how at this early stage of the attempt to draw her into the Army movement, I strenuously resisted it.

"CLAPHAM COMMON, 1st *May* 1882.

"My Dear Miss Booth,—I regret that I cannot sanction my dear child leaving school so soon after her return there. During the last two years there have been so many breaks in her school routine, that I am anxious this term should be passed studiously and tranquilly. Moreover, as I told you in my last letter, I am intensely anxious as to her present condition of mind, and I must keep her free from all excitement.—Believe me to be, yours very faithfully,

"SAMUEL CHARLESWORTH."

Other letters of a similar character were written by me, but all of no avail.

My anxious letters were said by Miss Booth to have called forth amusement in the "General," who jocosely remarked, "We must have a ward for lunatic Hallelujah Lasses at the Congress Hall, and Maud Charlesworth shall be the matron."

I must append one more extract, which is from a letter addressed to Mrs Booth, after I despaired of influencing the daughter. It is important, because it bears upon the marriage question, through my having then a faint suspicion that my child had been drawn into a feeling of attachment to one of the sons.

The letter was written from Ambleside, where I was staying for a short time with my children, and dated 12th September 1882:

"Some months since I wrote to Miss Emma Booth,

with reference to the effect which the Salvation Army work and meetings were producing upon my child. I found her so changed in character and conduct, so engrossed in the Salvation Army movement, as to be losing all interest in her friends and relatives, her home interests and associations, her studies and former pursuits; in fact, her whole mind and affections have become absorbed in the Salvation Army.

"The *War Cry*, and the letters she receives from her Salvation Army friends, engage every thought. This I have felt to be unnatural and dangerous to her health of body and mind. Therefore my letter written to your daughter, which I should be thankful for you to read, if it be not destroyed, as it will save me the painful effort of writing again the details which the letter contains. As a father, I have ever sought to have the entire confidence of my dear children. I have felt that true love and unreserved confidence must go together; that one cannot exist without the other. What I have thus desired to possess in my children, I have given to them in return. I trust them implicitly, consequently I never ask to see their letters, either written to or by them, so that I have never read a line of any communication passing between Maud and her Salvation Army friends. According to the rule adopted at her school, her letters have been always first enclosed to me unsealed; but I have, as she knows, in my confidence in her, forwarded them unlooked at. She has now been at home with me from school for six weeks. I have marked with painful and intense anxiety the all-engrossing and absorbing influence of the Salvation Army upon her. It is of so morbid a character she can turn to nothing else with interest or pleasure. Moreover, her excitement to get letters from her Salvation Army friends, and the *War Cry* is so intense, it must be harmful. Almost every day she is writing in reply. So long as this absorption, this excitement has only been the result of the religious feeling the Salvation Army movement has called forth, it has had my entire sympathy and met with no opposition. She has not been, as your daughter assumed in her letter to me, in a state of isolation in her family; on the contrary, we read and talk over your books together, and I have gone with her to your meetings in London. I have sought to understand the work, and to enter into her feelings. But some, who have known more than I have of what passes between her Salvation Army friends and herself, have warned me that there is another cause for all this absorption, that her affections have been called forth towards a gentleman, much her senior in years, who occupies a prominent position in the Salvation Army movement. This I could not credit, because any intercourse must have been most brief, and only at religious meetings. I could not assume that any Christian gentleman would avail himself of such an opportunity to draw forth the affections of a mere child, only sixteen years of age, unknown to her father; or that any Christian lady would, in her letters, encourage and foster such a feeling, if it had, consciously or unconsciously on the part of the gentleman, been drawn forth. So I strove to banish such a suspicion from my mind. However, the other day, Maud, on returning with me from an excursion, rushed up into the room where our letters would be found, and with an exclamation of joy carried off a letter to her bedroom.

"Observing her afterwards sitting at the window of our parlour, evidently under a feeling of intense emotion suppressed, I put my hand on her flushed forehead, and said, 'My dear child has had some letter that has disturbed her.' She replied, 'Oh no, papa, I have not.' Afterwards her sister informed me that the letter she had received was from the gentleman to whom I have referred, and that she had told her that she ought to show it to me. On a subsequent day, on receiving a letter from your daughter, she was found by her sister in an agony of grief in her bedroom, and she had a sleepless night of sobbing. The cause was, her sister learned from her, that this gentleman had been ill. It is with this knowledge, coming so unexpectedly upon me, as a blow of intense anxiety, that I write to you, dear Mrs Booth. I cannot speak to my child on the subject. It is the first breach of loving confidence between us. She is now too excited, too impulsive to be checked. If I were to thwart her in anything connected with the Salvation Army, it would alienate her from me, and from her home. I must leave the matter in your hands, to your motherly instinct and deep feeling, on behalf of my motherless child, remembering her youth, her inexperience. I cannot let her go back to school. I only can watch over her in this dark phase of her young life. No one must know of this but yourself; you must counsel me, you must aid me. My letter to your daughter will apprize you why I am so intensely anxious in my child's behalf. It is no selfish feeling of a father; but I feel that the dark cloud now gathering upon her bright young life may embitter the whole of our family happiness and peace. Please, not a word must be written or said to my child. So much judgment and caution and kindness will be needed in dealing with her."

I am precluded from inserting the replies of Mrs Booth and her daughter. My letters were then written to them with a desire that they should be private, their replies were consequently also marked private. I am at liberty to annul my own restriction, but not theirs. Suffice it to say the sum and substance, or the whole purport of their replies was, give your daughter up to active service in the Salvation Army, that will be the best antidote against injury to health of body or mind. But I received assurances from both mother and daughter that my anxiety as to Maud having any love attachment was perfectly groundless, for that the son in question was already engaged to be married to a young lady of large fortune, who was connected with the Army. Resting on these assurances, I afterwards made an arrangement for my child to be left temporarily under the care of one of the daughters in Paris; an arrangement I would never, for one moment, have entered into, but that I was thus lulled into false security. Six months after my letter to Mrs Booth, I for the first time learned from my child, that for more than a year and a half her affections had been thus drawn forth.

When I then appealed to Mrs Booth to tell my child that her son's affections were already engaged, she refused to do it; and a year after her letter to me, assuring me of the groundlessness of my suspicions, I received a letter from her husband, asking for my consent to my child's engagement to his son, which I of course refused.

Yet within a year from that time, though Miss Booth and my daughter had each given me a solemn promise in writing that she should not engage herself to any one without my consent, before she was of age, she nevertheless did engage herself to this same son, a man to whom I had never spoken, and of whom I knew nothing, and who at last came to me, two days before he sailed to Australia, with the endeavour to force me to consent to a marriage, on the ground that it was my wife's dying desire.

Since that refusal, nearly a year ago, I have not seen my child. I have received very bitter letters of reproach from her for thus destroying her happiness and undermining her health, but I think that no Christian parent, valuing the life-happiness of his child, would have consented to a marriage under such circumstances. Had I known the real character of the persons with whom I had to deal in those earlier transactions, I should have adopted a very different course. But when it is borne in mind that my child's reason was trembling in the balance, that her health was undermined, so that I was advised by the medical man, who had attended her at her school, to act with the greatest caution, and to keep her from all excitement and fatigue, I am sure that any parent who has undergone an ordeal of such a character, and who knows how hopeless a phase of insanity religious monomania is, will judge whether in seeking to pacify and calm my child by avoiding any forced subjection to my wishes, I did not pursue the wisest and best course at a time when she was in a frenzy of excitement of religious enthusiasm, mixed up with an attachment, drawn forth in the heated atmosphere of sensational services.

I copy here one letter which I wrote to my child when at school in answer to a letter from her, anxiously desiring that she might accept Miss Booth's first invitation.

17th March 1882.

"My beloved Child,—As dear Mrs * * * does not see it right or well to decide for us in a matter of so much anxious importance, the question must rest with me to decide as to the course I adopt. I could not leave such a subject to be determined by one of my other children. The reason why I wished to leave it to dear Mrs * * * is because she is in daily intercourse with you, and knows much more of your spiritual state and feelings than I know; moreover, I look upon her as your godmother, as now standing, as to your religious life, in the place of your dear mother. In looking back upon the past I am sure my dear child will feel that her father has loved her tenderly and strongly, ever desiring and seeking her welfare and happiness in things both spiritual and temporal.

"I have been drawn more towards you than to my other dear children through your illnesses at home, and because you have been more with me than they, as my little Limehouse companion; also because I have sympathised more than any one else in your schoolroom trials and discouragements, under the mismanagement and ill-judged treatment of governesses. Therefore I think I may claim from my dear child the confidence of one who loves her truly.

"The only cloud that has ever come between our love and sympathy and confidence has been the Salvation Army. Since my child associated herself with that movement she has not been the same to me, and I have not been the same to her; on her part, I am sure, she has been not only quite unintentionally, but unconsciously different. But the fact is, we are now in our religious life travelling two separate and distinct paths, choosing different companions and associations, and imbibing opposing sentiments and feelings. Her religious life or character receives its form and tone from the Booth family, mine still remains with the Church of which I am a minister, and with the people who are its members. That the holy earnest people from whom the Salvation Army had its origin have carried on a great and noble work in evangelising the poor and ignorant I have no doubt. You know that when the magistrates interdicted their preaching in the streets six or seven years since, I received them gladly into my garden for their Sunday afternoon services for several years. But now their religious work and character are totally changed; they have departed, as I consider, from the simplicity of the Gospel, and are adopting means which I regard as unscriptural, and of which I entirely disapprove. Sensationalism and excitement have taken the place of plain earnest teaching, and a vague unsatisfactory haze of truth and doctrine undermines the purity and scriptural character of their religious teaching and practice. I still regard Mr Booth and his family to be devoted earnest Christian workers, but I consider that they are building on the foundation of the Gospel much that seems to be of the nature of wood, hay, and stubble. My dear child thinks and feels on this subject very differently from her father, and she knows it, and deplores it, therefore the shadow of the cloud which has come between their love and confidence. As I said, both are now travelling on diverse paths, in the same road still, I trust, leading to the same goal, but not walking together or feeling in unison.

"I do not, my beloved child, exercise the authority of a parent to check or control you.

"The secrets of the soul in its life, growth, and aspirations are too sacred for a father to come between the soul and its heavenly Father; at least so long as I do not think that perilous error is imbibed, or that your soul's safety is endangered. Much as I grieve over our spiritual divergence, I will not, I cannot say to you, my child come to my side again, because I might thereby impede your spiritual growth or check your heavenward aspirations; also, I might at your age, with your great impulsiveness and keen sensibilities, do harm both to body and mind. I can only stand aloof with sorrow, and leave you in the hands of a gracious, all-wise, and loving Father, Saviour, and Sanctifier.

"Having said thus much, my dear child, I now leave you at liberty to accept or decline the invitation of Miss Emma Booth, only it must be entirely your act and not mine. You accept it. I do not, and cannot accept it for you. Your father's house is ever open to you as your home. Your father's love is ever wishing and seeking to shelter you from harm.

"Doubtless dear Florence will hope to see you during the holidays.—I am, my beloved child, ever your devoted affectionate father,

"SAMUEL CHARLESWORTH."

Before I close this chapter I may throw some light upon the failure of my efforts to induce Mrs Booth and her daughters to relax their hold upon my child, and to leave her to my care and guidance in her religious life and conduct, by quoting an extract from the report in the public journals, of a speech by Mrs Booth at a meeting held in Exeter Hall on 12th January 1885.

"Mrs Booth subsequently gave a stirring address, in which she deplored the refusal of parents and guardians to allow children or charges to leave the country in the service of the Salvation Army, and advised those young people who were led to offer themselves for this foreign work to go, whether or not they obtained permission of friends or relatives."

With this Salvation Army principle of ignoring the

rights and claims of parents and relatives entirely accords my own painful experience. It is not the question of yielding up children to the service of the Lord Jesus Christ, but of handing them over to the wild schemes of the Booth family in the service of the Army.

In my last interview with Mrs Booth more than a year since, when I made a most earnest appeal to her that she should use her influence over my child to induce her to return to me, she said, "I will not. You must remember that you are an old man, too old to expect that a young girl will care to be your companion; she desires more lively society."

CHAPTER IV.

THE Easter holidays of 1882 fully unfolded to me the influence which the Booth family had exercised and obtained over my child in calling forth her enthusiastic devotion to the Army; but I was then in entire ignorance of her attachment to one of the sons. I also knew nothing of two books which she possessed and studiously concealed from me, viz., the Army rules and regulations, and the Army doctrines and discipline—the latter book she had been specially enjoined when it was given to her not to show to anyone.

I had many conversations with her, in which she most earnestly entreated me to allow her to join the Army, on the ground that her spiritual life depended upon her uniting with them in religious communion, and that she felt sure the Army was her special call into the Lord's service. I endeavoured to show her that in her own previous home life, and in the services and teaching of the Church in which she had been brought up, she had hitherto found all she needed, and that she had been allured by the sensationalism and exciting services of the Army, rather than by finding Christ more fully manifested to her in that religious system. However, all argument, all persuasion were ineffectual. She ceased to take any interest in home pursuits and former friends, and in our Church services; her love for me and her eldest sister seemed to be fast waning; indeed I began to feel that I had no hold upon her affections, excepting when I showed an interest in books or subjects connected with the Army. At length, after fruitless efforts to win her back to her former interests and pursuits, in order to pacify her mind, and to allay the restless feeling pervading her daily life, I gave her a promise that if she would remain quietly at school, and diligently pursue her studies until she was eighteen, I would then leave her free to follow her own course of action; but I never in any form gave my consent to her actually joining the Army, either then or afterwards. I need hardly add, that if I had known the Booth family as I afterwards knew them, or had I known of her attachment to one of the sons, or had I known the contents of those two books withheld from me, I should never have given even the limited permission for her to follow her own bent. After the Easter vacation she returned to school. During the whole of the ensuing term she was absorbed in the Army work. She held prayer meetings with her young schoolfellows, feeling it to be her special mission to convert them and the household servants. Her letters to me told of the great work she was carrying on among them, and how day by day the Lord was giving her souls. Unknown to me she wrote to the whole circle of our relatives and friends, and to strangers for donations to the Army funds, by which she raised more than £50 in six months. It was during this term and the previous vacation that my letters were written to Miss Emma Booth in answer to her repeated invitations for Maud to go and stay with them. During this term I wrote anxiously to the friend under whose care she was placed, and I suggested that her correspondence with Miss Booth and her perusal of the *War Cry* should be stopped, but my friend demurred to this. I was still buoyed up with the hope that I should prevail upon the Booths to relinquish their hold upon her.

The term ended, my child returned home still more determinately resolved on joining the Army, more indifferent to all home associations and occupations, and seeming to feel less the bonds of affection binding her to me and her sister. Under the intense anxiety of this difficult position I determined to take both of my children a tour through the lake district, which they had never seen, hoping that the interest and variety of such an excursion might improve the bodily health of

Maud, and in some measure divert her thoughts from the Salvation Army. We went first to Wales and thence to Westmoreland and Cumberland, but the plan was an utter failure. Letters from her Army friends and the *War Cry* were objects of far deeper interest and attraction than mountains and lakes. In the steamboats, and when stopping to rest in our mountain ascents, the *War Cry* was drawn from the pocket and read with avidity. It was at this time that my letter, an extract from which has been given on pages 17-20, was written to Mrs Booth. In one town where we remained a fortnight the Army had a corps and barracks. I availed myself of this opportunity to watch the work thus carried on nearly 300 miles from head-quarters, and with that object I took Maud to some of the meetings. They were of the same character as those I had attended in London, only more rough and noisy. Sensation was the motive power, excitement the sustaining force. My feeling of objection to the system, as it regarded my daughter, was strengthened, and though I admired the earnestness and devotion of the young female captain and her girl helpers, I became more sensible of the harmful effect of such a mode of life upon the character of young enthusiastic girls away from parents, friends, and home-safeguards and restraints.

After two months I returned home very sorrowful and desponding. I began now to understand more thoroughly, the character of the Booths and their religious system, though they were still entirely unknown to me personally, except as correspondents; but I read in their letters the spirit and principles which actuated them. The Army was to be paramount to everything. Before its interests and advancement all home duties, social claims, relationship-bonds, and Church associations were to be as nothing.

Affections, sympathies, life duties and objects were all to yield to the Army call, or rather to be turned towards the Army and to be centred upon it, as the one great purpose, aim, and end of life.

Hopeless now of moving the Booths to relax their hold or to modify their influence; equally hopeless of turning the bent of my child's mind and affections again towards home duties and interests; and feeling it useless to send her back to school to pass another term in proselytizing and collecting money for the Army, I was perplexed as to what course I should adopt. Under this sorrowful difficulty as to the future, I adopted a plan which seemed to be worth a trial as the only one then at all feasible. I had read with much interest of the eldest Miss Booth's work in Paris, and had contributed to the funds for carrying it on. I was entirely unknown to her, and I believed that my daughter was also; at all events Miss Booth had been in no way to my knowledge a party in the influence which had been exerted over my child to induce her to join the Army.

In my great difficulty with regard to my child's state of health, mind, and body, the thought occurred to me, that if I placed her for a time under the charge of Miss Booth at Paris, merely as a young friend and visitor to help a little in the work among the Parisian poor, it would take her away from the harmful excitement of the work as carried on in London, and also guard her from personal intercourse with the son towards whom I now had reason to fear she was feeling, if not some attachment, yet a degree of enthusiastic admiration harmful to one so young and inexperienced, having regard to the fact of his being engaged to be married to another. With this purpose, somewhat indefinitely in view, I took her over to Paris, without mentioning my object to any one, staying at an Hotel not far from the Quai Valmy. I went with her for several evenings to the meetings held in the Army Hall there. Without introducing myself to the notice of Miss Booth, I sat quietly as an unobserved auditor closely watching the conduct of the meetings. I was greatly struck with the earnestness, simplicity, and devoutness which pervaded them, not only on the part of the three or four

English workers, but also of the French converts, of whom there were many. But what most called forth my interest and approval was the numbers of the lower class of the French people who came to worship and to listen. The sweetness of the hymn singing, the fervency of the prayers and addresses, and the absence of all sensational aids to excitement, gave me great confidence in this branch of the Army's work.

After attending thus several meetings and being most favourably impressed, I wrote to Miss Booth, mentioning without reserve the object of my visit to Paris, and requesting an interview at her residence. In that interview I stated more fully my great difficulty with reference to my child, my decided disapproval of much of the Army work as carried on in London, and my wish to withdraw my child from association with it.

I then proposed to leave Maud under the charge of Miss Booth as a young friend and visitor, to pursue her music and French and German studies, under the teachers who instructed Miss Booth's young English helpers; but I expressly stipulated that she should in no form be connected with the Army or wear the Army dress, but only be engaged in attending the meetings and in domiciliary visits upon the French poor in company with Miss Booth. I agreed to pay a stipend at the rate of £100 per annum for her board, lodging, and instruction. Miss Booth cordially entered into my plan, saying that she quite understood my feelings as to the objection of my child engaging in the work in England, and that with her she should be kept free from all excitement and fatigue. My daughter gladly became an assenting party to this arrangement. Being as conversant with the French language as with her native tongue, from having been always under the instruction of French or German governesses at home, and having been much abroad with her mother and sisters, she spoke with great facility and correctness of idiom. I arranged, that in case of her attending evening meetings with Miss Booth, she should always ride home with her in a closed carriage, it being the winter season; and I left with my child £5 to be expended for that purpose.

On parting with Miss Booth, I gave her a cheque, made payable to her, for £25 for the first quarter of the arranged stipend. *It will hardly be credited* that the cheque so given to her was forwarded immediately to head-quarters to be entered *as a donation* from me, the Rev. Samuel Charlesworth, to the Army funds, thus giving the sanction and support of my name as a London clergyman to the Army, though I had told Miss Booth how I disapproved of it. When six months afterwards I accidentally became aware of this misapplication, and remonstrated with her upon it, she said it was a mistake and she was sorry for it.

Before I left Paris, my dear child seemed to relent in her desire to be left with Miss Booth, and wished to return with me; but as the arrangement had been completed with her approval, and she had taken possession of her sleeping-room, and Miss Booth had acted upon it in allowing one or two of her young companions to take a short season of rest away from Paris, I felt that we could not honourably withdraw from the arrangement, and I counselled my child to remain for a little while at least.

The following letter written to her on the day of my return home will shew how I felt on this subject:—

"28*th November* 1882.

"My beloved Child,—Annie and I reached Belle Vue safely after a comfortable journey a little before 8 o'clock.

"I did not yesterday like, after what my darling Maud said to me, to urge her to remain in Paris, but it was a relief to me this morning to find, that she had decided to stay with dear Miss Booth; because I felt that she had honourably pledged herself to be her friendly helper for a time; and to draw back seemed to be a turning away from the Lord's work and purpose, after putting her hand to the plough. Therefore I am sure she did both wisely and bravely in resolving to remain, and the Lord will bless her for the self-denial. How often I shall think of my precious child, and picture all she is doing, and the comfort and help she is to her dear friend and her other companions. What a blessing you may be to those poor French people.

"When next I write I will send you a photograph.

"God bless you my dear child.—Ever your loving father,   SAMUEL CHARLESWORTH."

I returned home with the confident hope that the arrangement I had made, whilst it satisfied the yearnings of my child's ardent mind for work in the Army, would free her from the harmful influence of the excitement to which she had been subjected in the holiness meetings in London, and that her correspondence with the members of the Booth family would now cease, and her misplaced attachment, if such existed, would merge in the interest of her work in Paris, and in her association and new friendship with Miss Booth and her young companions and helpers. But this delusion was soon to be dispelled, and I was to find to my sorrow that the baneful influence of the Army system, like that of the Jesuit system of Rome, so infected every branch and every member of the society, that no faith was to be placed in the fairest appearances or the strongest assurances and promises.

I had not been home five weeks before I learned to my distress that my young delicate child had been sent out by Miss Booth, three miles away from her place of residence, to sell the French *War Cry*, the *En Avant*, in the streets of Paris in front of the Opera House, the Bourse, and the Madeleine, for hours at a time each day, and this towards the close of December. My poor child afterwards stated that she had sold 5000 copies herself.

The following is Mr Booth's description of what used to take place in the selling of the *En Avant*; it is extracted from the "Salvation War," 1882, page 104:—

"SELLING 'EN AVANT' IN THE STREETS OF PARIS.

"Three o'clock in the afternoon outside the Bourse (Stock Exchange of Paris), three English girls in full Salvation Army uniform, each wearing a large satchel slung across the shoulder well packed with French *War Crys*, holding two open they begin at once to work by saying in a loud, clear voice, '*En Avant*, un sou.'

"Their bright uniform and strange appearance attract attention. One man hurries towards them calling out to his companions, 'Why, what's this? What pretty little paper sellers! let's see what they've got.' One, now another, and then another, each with some fresh remark, looking the poor little English lieutenants up and down as if they could not believe they were ordinary beings.

"But the mid-day rush is over, there are only a few standing about and the passers-by; the sale of *En Avant* is very slow, only one here and there with many questions. One of the lieutenants inquires, 'Is it worth while staying? Is the business over for the day?' 'No, it commences again at six.' 'Hallelujah! we'll wait.'

"Walking up and down, first stopping at one entrance, then at another, calling out in all kinds of tempting ways, but still the people don't buy. Five o'clock strikes, carriages drive up, crowds of gentlemen appear from all quarters; now a quick sale. Rich as well as poor shall hear of Salvation! 'Do they buy?' No! only one here and one there. The wide flight of steps and pavement in front of the building is covered like an arena; but, instead of looking towards the building or entering in, they have all their eyeglasses up gazing at something. What? Three little English girls selling, or rather trying to sell, *En Avant*.

"At last one comes forward and buys, then another who says, 'Do you think I want this journal? No! it is only to please you that I buy it; your uniform amuses me, it is so charming, so attractive.' A little later on two others are overheard discussing very intently whether the seller of *En Avant* close by is English or German. Then comes along an old man, he buys one, and turning to two young men, calls out, 'Now then, get out your sous;' they have a good joke and then walk on.

"The cry of *En Evant* goes on a little longer; the sellers walk up and down, the crowds of gentlemen are still occupied in 'taking stock' with their eye-glasses. But now a little group have something else to look at; how intent they are! One man knocks another's elbow, attracting his attention to the announcements on the front sheet of *En Evant*. 'La Maréchale! A woman! What can it be?' We leave them to solve their difficulty with a prayer, and hope that it will lead them to the Hall. Now another comes up, saying with great enthusiasm, 'Why, I see you are taking the enemy by force!' Hallelujah! What encouragement in the midst of sarcasm, criticism, and gazing; it comes like a shower of rain on a thirsty land. Then others come questioning the sellers as to why they sell, &c. They are bravely answered that it is for God alone."

A gentleman who had lived thirty years in Paris, and who, therefore, knew well the tone of public feeling there, in kindly writing to warn me of the great objection to my daughter being thus exposed, cautioned me that girls selling newspapers on the pavements in Paris were regarded as of the most abandoned class.

The following is a letter I wrote to Maud on the subject:—

"CLAPHAM COMMON, 13*th January* 1883.

"My Dear Child,—When I read in the Salvation *War Cry*, 1882, page 104, the account of selling *En Avant* in the streets of Paris, I was so shocked and distressed at it; but I never for one moment supposed that my modest and gentle Maud would be found in front of the Paris Bourse, shouting out '*En Avant*, un sou,' and urging the libertine frequenters of that thoroughfare to buy a paper of her. I am grieved beyond measure, my child, to find that you have been doing this. I could not specify in my written conditions, on which I left you in Paris under Miss Booth's care, that you should not go into the streets to sell papers, because I could never dream of your engaging in such an unfeminine, indecorous work, but those conditions must have shewn that in principle I should be most opposed to such a step. What would dear mother or Aunt Maria or grandpapa have said could they have contemplated such a thing by their little Maudie. My dear child, whatever Miss Booth may feel it right to direct the officers under her to do, it would be wrong of me to oppose or question, but you are with her only as a guest—a young friend to assist her in her mission work, and you ought not to have been allowed thus to be exposed to those jeering, scoffing Parisians. I was grieved that Miss Booth left you in Paris, and I suppose it was after she left, you went out to sell papers. I wish now, my child, that you should return home to me, and I will come and fetch you, so soon as you come back to Paris. You have had full opportunity to see and engage in that noble and interesting work in Paris, and now I want my child with me, for I miss her much. Be sure to shew Miss Booth this letter.—Ever your loving father, "SAMUEL CHARLESWORTH."

But far worse troubles were gathering up. Miss Booth and her officers had planned to invade Switzerland, and she decided to take my child with her without writing to consult me or learn my wishes on the subject. Inasmuch as I had stipulated that my child was not to be separated from her, she therefore reasoned, as she afterwards explained to me, that the right course was to take her with her to Switzerland. As a father, I reasoned that the more correct course would have been first to consult me on the subject. But Army notions differ from parental. So my child, a girl of seventeen, was taken to invade Switzerland, and not only plunged into the thick of the war there, but made Miss Booth's right hand as secretary, keeper of accounts, and aide-de-camp, with the title of adjutant.

The following letter, written to my daughter, will best explain how I felt on the subject.

"CLAPHAM COMMON, 15*th February* 1883.

"My Dear Child,—I have been very grieved at the occurrences in Switzerland, both on your account personally and for the anxiety and distress it must have occasioned Miss Booth.

"When I left you in Paris, as a young friend and visitor under her charge, I had no conception that you would be put forward in the Army work as though you were an officer, nor had I any idea that you would be taken to Geneva. Your selling the *En Avant* in the streets of Paris was a great sorrow to me, but the position of publicity and prominence you have been allowed to take in Geneva is a far greater grief. It brings upon me much blame from all who know me, but who are ignorant of the real circumstances of the case, that I should be so imprudent as to let a daughter so young and inexperienced fall into such misadventure and be subjected to such treatment. As a clergyman, it brings upon me deserved reproach.

"The newspapers have spoken of you as almost a child. So you are in your knowledge of the world and the proprieties of public life. Those who love you among our relatives and friends are both shocked and surprised. And I do not wonder at such a feeling being excited, when they do not know how I have been placed. I should start for Berne directly, but I fear to miss you. As I am far from well, if I can avoid the long journey to Berne I shall be glad. But this must be as Miss Booth arranges, according to her convenience; her wishes must be studied. Endeavour, my child, to keep yourself from publicity and notoriety. Hereafter you will understand why this is necessary, as it affects yourself as well as your father and family. Miss Booth cannot retire from observation, because she is the responsible chief of the Army in Switzerland, and she must bear the trial of publicity.

"Let me know when and where I am to meet you, *by letter* if there be time, but if by telegram be sure to give the correct address; one I received was 'Clapton Common,' another was addressed only 'Charlesworth, Maitland, Clapham.' I wonder either reached me. Be sure to stay where you fix to meet me, so that I may not be journeying about in perplexity. May God our Heavenly Father guide and direct us all under these circumstances of sorrowful difficulty and anxiety.—Ever your loving father, "SAMUEL CHARLESWORTH."

Four days after writing this letter, I was startled on taking up the *Times* newspaper to read the following article:—

"THE SALVATION ARMY IN SWITZERLAND.

"Our Geneva correspondent writes:—
'Miss Charlesworth, who is now at Coppet, has been good enough to give me the following account of her expulsion and events which preceded it. Her artless narrative is both interesting in itself and valuable for the vivid light which it throws on the ways of Genevan justice—to foreigners. According to the *Journal de Geneve*, M. Heridier, Councillor of State charged with the Department of Justice and Police, was present at Miss Booth's and Miss Charlesworth's examinations, but behind a curtain, "after the manner of all Grand Inquisitors."

'"On Saturday afternoon," says Miss Charlesworth (who, it may be well to mention, is just sixteen years old), "a man came to the house of M. Lenoir, where we were staying, and said that Maud Charlesworth, aide-de-camp to Miss Booth, was to go at once and see the Chief of Police at the Hotel de Ville. I went at once, taking M. Lenoir with me, as I did not like to go alone. When we arrived M. Lenoir sent in to ask the Chief of the Police, M. Heridier, if he might be allowed to accompany me. We waited half an hour, and then the answer was that I must go alone. So there was nothing else for it, and I had to follow a savage-looking magistrate up stairs into a small and very hot office, where I was asked to sit down. I suppose they thought that this exceedingly cross-looking officer was not enough to question me, for two others, with equally unsaved (*sic*) looking faces, came in to help him. I had been with Katie (Miss Booth) both the times when she had to appear before the police, so I was quite prepared for the sort of questions they were going to ask me. The last thing Katie said to me was, 'Do not sign anything,' and I answered that I would sooner let my right hand be cut off; and when I got into that little room I made up my mind that when they came to the end and asked me to sign I would refuse unless they would allow M. Lenoir to come up and read the paper through.

'" Well, they began and asked me about the private meeting at which I had been present. They said it was a public meeting because three detectives had got in without being asked at the door for their cards of invitation. I denied the false statement, and made them write down my answer plainly. The point on which I laid the most stress was that we, the four Salvation officers, had been invited to a private meeting in a private house, to which others (strangers to us) had also been invited; that we spoke, prayed, and sang, as did others who did not belong to the Salvation Army, and that if people who were not invited made their way in it was not our fault; we were only guests. Then they asked me how I dared to wear my uniform at the meeting when I had been told of the law forbidding the wearing of a religious dress. Now; I know this law by heart. It says that no one is to wear a religious dress on the public highway. My answer was that I did not think the words 'public highway' could apply to the kitchen of a cottage in which a private meeting was held. I must here tell you that my questioners, or rather persecutors (of whom most of the time there were five), were very unsaved, and all possessed very quick tempers. Their object was evidently to frighten me so as to make me answer unwisely, and catch me in my speech. But they were disappointed, for they had never had to do with a Salvationist before, and could not make out why I was so calm and answered so clearly. They were also disappointed to find that I understood their language, and no matter how fast they read I was always ready with an answer. Every now and then one or another went into a passion. But the worst was to come.

'"'Have you got a passport or "leave to stay" in Geneva?' asked one of the crossest of the examiners (with whom I was now quite alone), and I could see by his manner that he thought I had not got my papers. I answered that I had my leave to stay, and that my passport was in the hands of the police. You should have seen the rage he got into. He rose, threw down his chair, stamped out of the room, shouted for some under officer, and asked the man what he meant by saying I was not provided with a passport. This man also lost his temper, went off to look for the passport, and in a few minutes returned and saw I was quite right, that they had my passport and I my 'leave to stay.' The inspector then flew into a greater rage than before, and scolded the man who had misled him. When he was more composed he continued. But now he came to personal questions, which I told him he had no right to ask, and I enquired what law authorised him to ask them. He said that was not his affair; he had been told to ask these questions, and I must answer. He asked me if I had my father's leave to remain at Geneva, and when I said 'Yes,' he wanted letters to prove it. I asked him how he dared to doubt my word, and told him to write down that Miss Booth had letters from my father authorising me to stay. A little later he said that I had prayed in a private meeting according to the form of the Salvation Army. I insisted that the Salvation Army had no form of prayer, and asked him in what way their prayers differed from other prayers. He said they differed very much, but he could not tell me how; he repeated we had a form of prayer, and began to storm and rave so loudly that an inspector ran in from the next room, saying, 'Gently, gently, there is somebody outside.' ... At last, after a great deal more questioning, my paper was finished. I knew all my answers were true, and that there was no harm in putting my name to it; but then I remembered my promise to Katie, so I refused, unless I might go down and fetch M. Lenoir, and I said I would not sign the paper until he had read it. Of course they raved at me, but it had no effect; so they went for M. Lenoir, but unfortunately he had gone away, as they came back in triumph to tell me. I still refused to sign, and said I would not sign until 'Captain' Bouilatt (a member of the Salvation Army) had read it through. They were angry, and tried to frighten me, all talking as fast as they could at the same time. Then they said they would read the paper all through again, which they did three times; but nothing could move me. I said I would go with Zitza and fetch Bouillat. They answered that I might go, but not with Zitza (a Salvationist, who was waiting to be examined), but I said I could not think of such a thing—that it would be very improper for a young lady to walk through the streets after dark, especially as I knew there was a plot on foot to do us harm."

In the end two gendarmes were sent for Bouillat, Miss Charlesworth and Zitza waiting meanwhile in the little hot office.

'"All at once it struck me," she continues, "that we would have a prayer meeting. 'Zitza,' I said, 'we will pray. Let us go down on our knees and pray for these people, for if ever we wanted the Lord with us it is now.' So down we went and prayed out loud for about ten minutes, and it did us good. The inspector was much surprised; he cleared his throat, grunted, and finally got up and went to the door of the outer office. Then four of the men came back. I said to Zitza that we would tell the Correspondent of the *Times*, and that I wondered what the English would think of the way in which their countrywomen were being treated. This was overheard, and seemed to make an impression, for two men came and said I was quite free to go if I liked, or if they could fetch me anything they would do so. I wanted to fetch Bouillat, but when I found that I should either have to go alone or walk between two policemen, I preferred to wait."

At length Bouillat came, and on his recommendation she signed her deposition.

'" The great fun was," she goes on, " that all these cross magistrates and inspectors were kept from their dinners. So were we; but as I told them, that was a very secondary consideration to us. We left that office at half-past seven singing 'Glory to His Name.' I had been there four hours. The whole town knew it. A lawyer at once took all that had passed down in French, because he was so indignant.

'" On Sunday I received a paper which told me that before six o'clock I was to be out of the Canton, because, first, I had broken the law by speaking in a public meeting (lie No. 1); secondly, because I had nothing to show that my parents consented to my being with Miss Booth (lie No. 2.); thirdly, because that morning I had not appeared when sent for by the police. (We sent a letter to say that we could not go on Sunday.)

'" Before the man who brought this letter went away I made him tell me who else was expelled, and I found that Bouillat, Zitza, and Emile (all foreigners) had shared the same fate. We sent for them to come up that we might arrange where to go, but they did not come, and we found that they had been fetched out of their room, put into a cab with a policeman, and driven away without a moment's notice. So these three are gone, I know not whither, and Miss Booth sent a Swiss lass with me, as, of course, I could not go alone." ' "

I at once conferred with my other children, and with some near relatives whose judgment I valued, and we came to the unanimous conclusion that it was incumbent upon me to write to the Editor of the *Times* to express my regret that my child should have been implicated in such proceedings, and should have written such a letter, the tone of which I so entirely disapproved. I accordingly penned the following letter :—

"*To the Editor of the 'Times.'*

"Sir,—I have been greatly distressed this morning on reading in the *Times* an account purporting to have been given by my daughter, Maud Charlesworth, to your Geneva Correspondent respecting the part which she has been so unwisely allowed to take in the proceedings of the Salvation Army in Geneva.

"I feel it to be due to myself as a clergyman and to my family to ask your permission to state briefly the circumstances under which my youngest daughter has been so unfortunately mixed up with these proceedings of the Army. I ask this favour of you, because her name, during the past fortnight, has appeared so prominently in the *Times* in the intelligence items from Switzerland.

"Twelve years since the Rev. William Booth was carrying on a most useful, successful work in the East of London by means of an organisation called the Christian Mission, originated and supported by him. One of the principal stations being in my then parish, the work drew forth the interest and sympathy of myself and my family.

"A few years later Mr Booth adopted a different organisation and plan of operations in carrying on his work, an alteration in which I could not accord when it assumed its present form of the Salvation Army. About two years since, my daughter, then in her sixteenth year, was taken to some of the London meetings of the Salvation Army, and there introduced to members of Mr Booth's family. Being of a very impressible and somewhat excitable nature, deeply imbued with strong religious convictions and feelings, the Salvation Army took a strong hold upon her imagination, and she became fascinated with its meetings and work. Eventually she was so absorbed in the movement that all other interests seemed entirely to merge in her conception of the importance of the Christian work carried on by the Army. When I first became aware of the intense absorption and enthusiastic feeling to which she had yielded I was alarmed for the consequence, both as to health of body and mind. I saw it was needful that I should act most cautiously with her, and I accompanied her to two or three of the Army holiness meetings, that I might judge for myself of their effect upon her.

"I shrank with trembling from the responsibility of allowing a child of so sensitive a nature and impulsive a disposition to be subject to the intense excitement called forth in those meetings, the whole work being so essentially based and carried on by exciting appeals to the feelings. But I found with sorrow that my daughter had been already so wrought upon by the system that no other form of worship satisfied her spiritual cravings.

"Mr Booth's family were entirely unknown to me. I wrote to two of them with whom my daughter seemed most associated, very earnestly appealing to them not for the present, while she was so young and a schoolgirl, to do anything which would tend to encourage the excitement or the all-engrossing influence of the Army meetings and work. I regret to say that my appeal met with no responsive sympathy—indeed, I must add that, both with respect to my child and to other young persons of whom I have heard, I fear the Army influence has a direct tendency to wean the converts from home associations and interests, under the idea that its work is paramount in importance to all other pursuits and obligations, and even to the known wishes of parents. At all events, I then discovered, to my deep sorrow, that one of the most loving and devoted children had found stronger interests and more absorbing pursuits in the arena of the Army than in her own home.

"In the very painful dilemma in which I was placed with a motherless daughter to watch over, feeling that my child's happiness, and health of body and mind, probably depended upon her continuance in the Army work, and yet dreading the excitement of the work as carried on in London, I took her to Paris, having the impression that the work among the Parisian poor was of a less exciting character. I attended several meetings, and was greatly pleased with the earnestness of all the workers, and the moderation and propriety which pervaded all the proceedings under the superintendence of Miss Booth.

"By my daughter's desire I arranged with Miss Booth to leave her for a time in Paris, that she might assist Miss Booth in her arduous work among the poor; but expressly stipulating that she was only to be regarded as a young friend and visitor, and that she should not become an officer of the Army or wear their uniform.

"Shortly afterwards Miss Booth went to Geneva to open a station there, and took my daughter with her. Thus she has been so injudiciously and to me most lamentably placed in the very forefront of an aggressive movement in a foreign land; not only in direct contravention to both the letter and spirit of my express stipulations, but also opposed to the course which ought to have been taken, even if unexpressed, with reference to one of such tender age and so inexperienced. Any judicious parent reading the statements contained in the *Times* on the Geneva proceedings must have felt what a sorrowful and unwise position that young Christian girl had been drawn into.

"With regard to the Salvation Army itself, which is the real and principal question of public importance, and of interest to your readers, I wish I could be silent. So long as I could do so conscientiously I heartily desired to note only the good it effected, and to be silent on what might appear to me its defects or mistakes. It has undoubtedly been accomplishing a great work in the conversion and reformation of thousands of the most ignorant and depraved. But, in common with many of my clerical brethren and Christian friends, I now tremble for its future, because there seems to be creeping into it so much of the material and worldly element, as though in its great success and widespread influence the self-sacrificing and self-ignoring spirit were giving place to autocratic rule and exacting obedience—even the spirit of Rome and of the Jesuit order, in a modified form, superseding the spirit of love and humility. I have come reluctantly to this conclusion, the result in part of observing closely its present mode of operation, but more especially from learning the avowed doctrines and principles upon which its government and mode of procedure are based, as distinctly set forth in the printed code of orders and regulations drawn up for the guidance of the officers of the Army.

"I am most deeply pained and grieved to write this letter, but the publicity given to my young daughter's position and proceedings in the Army operations at Geneva seems to me to demand such an explanation, if it be only as a caution to other parents.

"I have the honour to be, Sir, your very obedient servant, "SAMUEL CHARLESWORTH."

"CLAPHAM COMMON, *Feb.* 19."

In acknowledgment of this letter I received the following courteous note from the Editor:—

"*February* 22nd, 1883.

"The Editor of the *Times* desires to thank Mr Charlesworth for his most interesting and useful letter, and to condole with him on the sorrow with which he has been visited. The Editor hopes that the result of this publicity, however painful it may seem at the moment, will be to restore Miss Charlesworth to the guardianship of her friends."

The following is a verbatim copy of a telegram sent

from the Army head-quarters in London to my daughter at Lausanne, the same morning on which my letter appeared in the *Times* :—

"Sightless father's letter to-day's *Times* saying paganism remain send messenger Geneva pellucidness. *Times'* correspondent doubtful letter abdicating collateral adoring."

I was not versed in the Army's telegraphic code, but I could read sufficiently between the lines of this telegram to judge that it was not such an one as a young daughter should have received concerning her father, an aged clergyman.

I afterwards learned from her that her alleged communication to the Correspondent of the *Times* was a most strictly private letter written to her "dear General." In her enthusiasm she of course gave a version of the affair after *War Cry* fashion, never deeming it would be made public. She sent it to Miss Booth to be forwarded to her father. Miss Booth being at Geneva, handed over the letter to the correspondent of the *Times*. He being put in possession of so racy and graphic an episode in Salvation Army warfare, telegraphed it to the *Times* office, therefore its appearance in the columns of that journal.

The following extracts from the Army's Orders and Regulations will explain why Miss Booth, as a commanding officer of the Army, gave up the private letter of her young secretary and aide-de-camp to the Correspondent of the *Times*.

Part 1, section 8, page 69. Use of Newspapers.

"Notices in newspapers of any kind are always of great service. A capable commanding officer will therefore take care to be published in them as soon as possible.

"There are often correspondents, local gossips, &c., whose business it is to collect and write in a taking way reports on novelties, entertainments, &c., &c.

"It is well worth while to take pains, and even spend a little money, if needs be, in obtaining such notice, for, even if they write violently against us, the result is increased attendance and benefit.

"Newspapers live very largely by controversy, and therefore editors are almost always fond of putting in letters advocating or condemning anything.

"Moreover, when there are several papers in a town they oppose each other, so that correspondence in one is very likely to cause some of a contrary kind in another.

"It is to the interest of the service to be in the columns as often as possible, no matter in what way.

"A commanding officer who does not get newspaper attention at the outset of the work will throw away an opportunity which will never return of benefiting the whole Army, and of keeping it before a very helpful class who are more to be influenced thus, than in any other way."

When I afterwards at Lausanne expressed my great regret to Miss Booth that my child's private letter should have been made public, she said it was a mistake and she was sorry for it, but nevertheless she could make no allowance for my own letter to the *Times*, which called forth upon me a storm of abuse from the supporters and partisans of the Army in numerous anonymous letters, platform addresses, and other forms of attack.

I will here insert a letter written by Miss Booth to me the day after the *Times* with my letter had reached her, to show how she regarded my communication. The italics show Miss Booth's underlining.

24th February 1883.

"Dear Mr Charlesworth,—Dear little Maud was ill yesterday. It was all I could do to comfort her; she seemed passed it. I am very troubled about her health. I fear for the strain on her brain—she was so much *better*. Her appetite another thing, and sleeping so well; but I could not wonder at her suffering, she seems as much at a loss to interpret it as I am, poor child; she was and is so distressed. It was not till evening, when we knelt down together, and placed the matter into His hands, who knows all from beginning to end, that she was at all comforted. I put my little one to bed, and kissed her for 'some one else,' and she was calm. The sweet little face looked so troubled: and indeed I am only *stunned*. Can it be possible that your child is made out to have acted a lie, to be *untrue*, when I, who have lived with her, have never seen the *slightest deviation* from the *straight line of truth!* Never *anything* that was inconsistent. That letter (which I so much regret the publication) was only, as the Correspondent of the *Times* said, beautiful *for its simplicity and straightforwardness; childlike!!* and now that all the world is to think she *misrepresented* the facts, and the whole thing was otherwise to what it *really was!* I cannot believe it. If they did but know *her*, but *One does*, and all the universe will know *one day*. Whatever you may think of the Salvation Army, bear in mind that it is an affair of *conscience* with your child, and has a right at least to be *respected*. To say she has been influenced (as probably her friends do say) is not true. It was all settled with Maud long before *I saw her*. She was *unknown* to me (having only once shaken hands with her in Exeter Hall in the crowd) until we met in Paris; and indeed her convictions were *so strong* that it would have been impossible to move her even if I would. Maud is fully decided to be true to her convictions, to give her life to the Lord. May I ask has she not a right, or as much a right as her sister, to marry.

"But I am more pained than I can say over all this. If you had wished your daughter to return, why did you not write so. Why did you not write to me about being unwilling for her to stay in Genèva? The *Times* states that Maud is in Genèva *without your authorisation and against your wish!* I should *never* have taken her under such circumstances. No one regrets *Maud's name* being in print as I do; but it *sounds* that she has been acting and taking part as she has not; *i.e.*, never been in such a scene as at Rue Oberkampf; and been *with me night and day*. Oh I am so grieved, can't understand *it at all*, and grieve for the darling child, not strong naturally, and, as you truly write, *excitable* and highly strung; therefore needing *wise and careful* treatment. I tremble for the result of this on her delicate frame, and I am glad to be near her. As you love her, let me ask you to write her by return of post, and put her mind at rest. I have heard fear expressed for her brain, and the course adopted lately seems the *surest* to bring about the result (terrible indeed). I write this in confidence, and only to you her father. I am interested in her, and God knows, only seek to lead her in the straight path of holiness, to follow her precious mother. I feel I must, and may, in some small way fill her place. I understand your child, I know what she needs, and have been *very* firm in insisting on a certain course, when I've seen it necessary. Maud has *yielded* to my judgment on these points. That she is enthusiastic is not *sin*. She only needs some one just now who *understands and loves her to guide;* and as I told you in a former letter she will be yet a bright gem for the Lord, and many poor souls will have reason to bless God for having heard her. But to withstand her, to *force her*, to persuade her, *to be unfaithful to her convictions is a dangerous course* in a spiritual point of view, as well as physical. Does any one doubt her being led by the spirit of the Lord? I have nothing to say to these. To speak of her being weaned from her family, from you, does rouse me, and make me once more pray that patience may *have her perfect work!* Am I weaned from my family? Have I abandoned my father, as the French journal *says she has done?*

"No child ever spoke in more loving terms of her father than yours. She never mentions your name but in the highest terms! This makes the blow double.

She said always, 'My father understands me if my sister does not;' 'My father loves me;' and she has counted always on that love! For your child's sake I ask you to be careful, at the risk of being *misunderstood* (need I write that word *to you*, it seems as if I *was* to be misunderstood and my motives misconstrued). I ask that you will not hurry Maud away; leave her with me. I am coming to England in a fortnight's time. I can take her out in the fields; there are some lovely quiet walks, and the mountains and scenery are charming. We have already taken some walks. It has been such a treat. For her to be placed among friends *just now*, to hear all *they have to say!* their different opinions, &c., might cause *a serious illness*, resulting in what I cannot write! I can *turn her attention* from this painful subject, quiet her; and she will, I trust, return the bright child she has been while with me. Excuse this bad writing, I am tried very much, and my back pains me. Maud may have written, *she is a little better now*. I ask you to think over what I've written. I have Maud's *truest interest at heart;* and her future health and life, I feel, are at stake.—Yours grieved,

"CATHERINE BOOTH."

I have inserted this extraordinary and to me unsatisfactory letter at length verbatim, inasmuch as it is Miss Booth's justification of the mode in which she had carried out the trust I had reposed in her. I must comment on its incorrect statements. I had previously before this occurrence written saying that my child must return home to me; but having a letter from Miss Booth earnestly entreating I would allow her to remain, and warning me that her health of body and mind would be imperilled if I compelled her to come home, I yielded reluctantly to her continuing with Miss Booth. In the foregoing letter, her state of health is attributed entirely to my letter to the *Times*. Miss Booth is unmindful of my child's daily exposure in the month of December, for hours in the streets of Paris, selling the *En Avant*. She is unmindful of the journey she took her from Paris to Geneva in the depth of winter; she is unmindful of her exposure in Switzerland to the cold night air on coming out of small, crowded, heated rooms; she is unmindful of all the excitement my child was dragged through in the conflicts with the police. Whatever illness she then had, or might as a consequence have, was to be attributed to my letter. However, all these apprehensions of illness were, as I afterwards found, illusory. Again, Miss Booth charges me with writing about my child in that letter to the *Times* as untruthful. This is a pure invention. I never for one moment, as will be apparent, thought or wrote of my child as being untruthful. The father, in writing to the *Times*, gave exactly the same incorrect impression of my letter, just in order to throw upon me the odium of accusing and blaming my child; whilst my only accusation was against those who had so wantonly led her into the false and imprudent position which she had occupied in Switzerland, as detailed in the London journals.

I had received from Miss Booth or her officers the most earnest requests that I would write to the English ambassador at Berne, to state that my child was with Miss Booth with my consent, because he refused to move in any way on behalf of the Army without such an assurance. I wrote a letter to the effect that, as she had been taken there, she then remained in Switzerland with my consent, but adding that she was with Miss Booth only as a young friend, to be in no way connected with the Army or its proceedings. The first part of my letter was published in the London and Swiss journals, the last qualifying portion being omitted. Again Miss Booth wrote to ask if my child was to remain in Switzerland. I expressed a wish that if she did remain, she should be placed under the care of a valued friend of mine at Lausanne, a lady totally unconnected with the Army. The first part of my letter was, in like manner, published, omitting the expressed wish that she should be placed under the care of my friend, with whom I intended she should stay, until I could go to Switzerland to fetch her home. Thus my letter was so quoted as to make it appear that I wished her to remain only with Miss Booth.

So it was in all quotations from letters and references to them; a portion only was given seeming to justify a course of action, which, had the entire letter been set out, it would have showed just a contrary intention and direction. When such means are resorted to, it is impossible to carry on fairly a newspaper correspondence. Editors will not insert long explanations in order to set straight misquotations, such merely personal details are of no interest to the general public. I may be pardoned for inserting here a letter, previously, on the very date of Miss Booth's letter, written to my child, as it in part anticipates or rather meets Miss Booth's incorrect statements:—

"CLAPHAM COMMON, 24*th February* 1883.

"My Beloved Child,—Your two letters came to me together this morning, Saturday, because your first letter with Miss Booth's being misdirected has been wandering about Clapton after me. Be sure in future always to address to me, as I have written above. My darling, we are indeed passing through troubled waters; I could not dream that the *Times*' Correspondent had not been requested and authorised by you to put in that sorrowful account, because he spoke of it as expressly communicated by you to him. I was so distressed at the tone of the account, looking at it as a public document. It was so unlike you, where the words 'unsaved faces,' 'great fun,' 'lie No. 1' occur. But for that sad document sent all over the world with the *Times* comments upon it, I should never have written my letter. But my position as a clergyman, and a father, forbad silence, especially as your Christian name was given. My dear child, all this trouble between us has arisen through your not carrying out my directions. You have allowed yourself to be put forward as the secretary and aide-de-camp of the Marèchal, and you have worn the uniform. Thus you have been thrust into a prominent position, which one so young (they have always spoken in the papers of your age as sixteen) should not have occupied. General Booth, in writing to the *Times* in reply to my letter, said, 'I am placed in an extremely delicate position, when a father, in order to condemn the Salvation Army, represents his daughter to the world as undutiful and untruthful.' This made me so sorrowfully indignant, because it was so utterly contrary to the fact, there was no ground for saying it; indeed, it was a pure invention. I would have cut off my right hand before I would have held up my darling child to the world as undutiful and untruthful. Yet General Booth has given you and me this character. There are several things he implies in his letter which are contrary to the fact, that I had inferred you were in Geneva contrary to my will. Nothing in my letter implied that. It was only that you were engaged as an officer and wearing their uniform that I objected to. My beloved child, these things are all very painful. Oh, would that my beloved child had remained quietly at home with me until she was eighteen; but then I saw how her mind and heart were with the Army, and I could not bear to feel she was pining for work with them, whilst I was keeping her in a home that had lost its chief interests and attractions.

"My dearest child, the clouds hovering over us throw very dark shadows, but let us remember that the sun of God's love shines beyond, and he can and will bring good and blessing out of the seeming evil. How near we are to Heaven if we did but know it, for His presence is Heaven, and His felt love is Heaven's chief joy and glory. I used to think Limehouse Rectory a very dull house when my Maudie was not there, but now the whole world seems dull to me because I have lost her. My child, I would never keep you from the Lord's service in any form, but I would keep you from street exposures and encounters, and from Police Courts, and danger of imprisonment, and I do from my heart solemnly question and doubt whether the practices of the Army are in accordance with the mind and will of Jesus. They stir up so much strife, and beget so much opposition, and create so much ill-feeling. Moreover, the great excitement of their meetings, as held in England, is so harmful to sensitive imaginative minds. Oh if they could only keep from these ebullitions, how noble a work they might carry on. I allow all the great good they have done, but now I see so much danger of evil mixing with the good. God grant it may not be so.

"And now, my child, as to the future, until you are eighteen, what is to be done? Write and suggest to me. Will you return to dear Belstead until then? May God guide and direct us. Do you not want more pocket money. I hope Miss Booth keeps account of all payments made for you.

"God Almighty bless you, my beloved child. I have to preach to-morrow at Croydon. To-day is dear little Magdelen's birth-day.—Ever in fond love, your devoted father, "SAMUEL CHARLESWORTH."

CHAPTER V.

The statements of Miss Booth in her letter relative to my daughter's precarious condition of health led me to set off immediately for Switzerland. I left the day I received it. The following letter, written to my child as I stopped for a night on the journey, will show how I then felt with reference to her:—

"MONTEREAU, *27th February* 1883.

"My Beloved Child,—I did not receive your and Miss Booth's two letters until yesterday (Monday) about twelve o'clock, as I had been absent from Clapham assisting a friend on Sunday. I was so grieved to hear from Miss Booth that you were ill. I do not wonder at it, the sorrow and worry of the last two weeks must have been terrible to bear. As soon as I could start I left home, in order that I might come and be near to you. But I am so far from well that I cannot travel far in one day, so I shall not reach Lausanne until Thursday afternoon. I will write to you, my dear child, when I am settled there, and then you can come and see me on Friday. I am not coming, my child, to take you home until you can be spared, as I do not wish to hinder justice being obtained from the officials at Geneva, but I am so anxious about you, I cannot bear to be far away from you, and at least I can be near to watch over you. Doubtless you know that the people at Geneva are greatly incensed at your letter. Official men cannot bear to be made to appear ridiculous before the public, however much they may have deserved it. Oh that the letter you wrote had never been published; then all our sorrow would have been avoided but for that. I should never have written to the *Times*, but after that appeared I could not avoid writing, painful as it was to me to do so. Oh my darling child, would that I had come for you when I last wrote to say I must, but your letter was so sorrowfully full of entreaty that I would not, that I refrained. My darling, I was so grieved that you should speak of wishing that you had died when you had the fever. God has had a great work for you to do for Him already, and I am sure He has a blessed work in reserve, and when His servants so murmur as Elijah and Jonah did at their trials, it displeases Him. Joseph when he was in the prison might have said, would that I had died when I was cast into the pit, but I do not think he did, for he trusted in his God at all times. Often when God has some great work for His servants to do, and frequently when He is about to pour down upon them a special blessing, He brings them through a season of distress to exercise their faith and patience. So it may be with you, my dear child. I must not write longer, for I am sitting in a cold damp room of a miserable little inn, and I feel very wearied.

"God bless you, my beloved child, and keep you near to Him. At some future day you may know why all this trial has happened, and oh that a blessing may come out of the seeming evil. I never, my child, said anything about you, but what the most loving father might say—not a word about anything like untruthfulness. Nothing that I said could be so interpreted. Ever your devoted father.

"SAMUEL CHARLESWORTH."

I reached Lausanne on Thursday afternoon, 1st March, and wrote to my child to come *alone* to see me on the following morning. I felt that I could not see Miss Booth after her letter to me of the 24th.

In the morning my child came to me. I then found that the statements as to her alarming condition of health were groundless—she was looking and feeling quite well, but of course greatly distressed in mind. In our interview I for the first time ventured to speak to her on the subject of the rumours I had heard as to her attachment to one of Mr Booth's sons. She acknowledged that her affections had been drawn forth towards him, through conversing with him on her spiritual state at the Salvation Army meetings, but that she had never spoken to him or seen him on any other occasions. This filled me with great sorrow on her account, as I had been so positively assured by the mother and sister of that son's engagement to another young person connected with the Army. I now decided to take my child home with me at once, and walked with her to the house where she was staying with Miss Booth, whom I declined to see. I arranged that we would leave for England on the following morning. I then went for a long walk, hoping by the effort to shake off in some measure my depression from the burden of anxiety which pressed so heavily upon me.

On returning to the hotel, the waiter told me that a young lady was waiting in the salon to see me. Supposing it to be Maud, I at once went into the salon, and had passed to the upper end of the room before I recognised Miss Booth sitting at a table writing. The mistress of the hotel was in the salon playing on the piano. I could not retreat. I felt also that in the presence of the hotel mistress I ought not, in courtesy, to request Miss Booth to leave the hotel, though she had come there knowing that I had declined to have any interview with her.

She at once said she hoped I would listen to a few words of explanation she had to offer. She mentioned that my letter in the *Times* had been inserted in a French religious publication *Le Christianisme*, the editor of which had commented upon it in a strain unfavourable to the Army, and that Pastor Theodore Monod of Paris had written to her for an explanation. She then assured me that the statements which had appeared in the London journals as to Maud bearing the title of an Army officer, wearing the uniform, and acting as her secretary and aide-de-camp were incorrect, and she entreated me to write a letter to Mr Monod authorising him to correct the misstatements of the journals. At first I refused, saying that the correction must be made by her or some one connected with the Army who could vouch for its accuracy; but, shedding tears, she appealed so very earnestly to me on the ground of the injury done to her work in Paris, that at last I yielded and wrote the following letter, grounded solely on her own assurances to me:

"The Rev. Pasteur Theodore Monod.

"Dear Sir,—Miss Booth has placed before me a number of *Le Christianisme*, 2nd March 1883, in which there are statements very painful to her, not so much in affecting herself personally as being prejudicial to the work in which she is engaged. These statements are founded on assertions made in the London journals which have been explained to me by my daughter and Miss Booth as having arisen in error of the true circumstances of the case. My daughter was not acting in the capacity of secretary or aide-de-camp to Miss Booth, and she did not wear the uniform of the Salvation Army, but only a dress made in England, of which I approved. When Miss Booth found it necessary to go to Geneva she was right in taking my daughter with her, as I had stipulated she should not be separated from Miss Booth, and being there, it was with my consent she remained. Miss Booth has watched over her and cared for her, and the unfortunate circumstances which have occurred in Geneva have arisen from the action of the authorities there and not from any intentional disregard by Miss Booth of the terms under which my daughter was left in her care. All these painful misunderstandings have originated through the letter written by my daughter to General Booth to be seen by him alone, but which through inadvertence was made public. You have my authority to use this letter in justification of Miss Booth.—I have the honour to be, dear Sir, yours very faithfully,

"S. CHARLESWORTH."

"LAUSANNE, *2nd March*, 1883."

It will hardly be credited that a copy of this letter was immediately, the same evening, sent off for publication in the Geneva journals, before the original was even posted to Pasteur Monod. When I, in ignorance of this having been done, was the following Tuesday conferring with Pasteur Monod in Paris as to the desirableness of his writing to the editor of *Le Christianisme* on the subject of my letter on that very day, a coloured translation of that letter was circulating in several journals throughout Switzerland as a retraction by me of my letter to the *Times*. I afterwards learned that my daughter *had really borne* the title of an Army officer, being recognised and addressed as adjutant, that she had acted as Miss Booth's aide-de-camp, secretary, and accountant, and that her dress was in accordance with her assigned position in the Army.

Three times on that Friday afternoon and evening Miss Booth came to my hotel on the subject of this letter, desiring corrections to strengthen its statements. On the last occasion she said that she had a special favour to ask of me. She was obliged to return to Paris the following morning, Saturday, by express train; she was feeling too ill to journey alone; none of her comrades could be spared to accompany her, would I kindly allow Maud to travel with her. I consented, but expressly stipulating that should they reach London before I did, Maud should be sent home at once to Clapham. To shew to Miss Booth the importance of her not taking Maud with her to Clapton, I explained to her what Maud had confessed to me about the brother, who was then living at home at Clapton. Miss Booth promised that she should go to Clapham. What follows will hardly be credited. Having arrived in Paris on Sunday, they started for London by the first train on Monday morning. On arriving at the Cannon Street Station at 5 o'clock, Miss Booth at once drove off with Maud to head-quarters in Queen Victoria Street, sending off a telegram to her father at Sheffield to the effect—" All right; arrived safely, Maud Charlesworth going home to Clapton; her father satisfied"—and then went off with her to Clapton. On my afterwards remonstrating with Miss Booth on her not having fulfilled her engagement with me, she said she was very sorry, that it was a mistake; that as no one came to meet Maud at Cannon Street, she did not know what to do with her, and took her home. She could send my child out in the streets of Paris, three miles off their home, to sell the *En Avant;* she could let her be exposed to arrest by the police authorities in Switzerland, and be conveyed by officers to the Geneva Frontier, on her forcible expulsion from the Canton; but in London, she could not send her in a cab from Cannon Street to Clapham, though there were many persons, male and female, at head-quarters, who could have gone with her. Moreover, having by such rapid travelling anticipated my arrival in England, she ought to have telegraphed from Calais or Dover to Clapham, when my eldest daughter, expecting to have some such communication, would have gone at once to meet her sister. *Those four days spent at Clapton demoralized my child;* then and there she was completely alienated from me and all her relatives; that first visit, so surreptitiously accomplished, changed the character of my child—from that time she was irrecoverably lost to me, and her home, and the Church of her youth.

On the same Monday evening, "General Booth" was presiding over a great Army meeting at Sheffield. At the commencement of the meeting he had been greeted with cries, "Where is Miss Charlesworth." The telegram arrived most opportunely, he read it to the meeting, saying, as reported in the papers, "that the dear good clergyman had received an explanation; was perfectly satisfied; was reconciled to the Army, and had allowed his daughter to go home with Miss Booth to Clapton."

Being too ill to travel home, excepting by slow stages, I did not reach Clapham until Thursday evening. I was astonished not to find my child there. My eldest daughter explained to me, that immediately on hearing that Maud had returned to England and gone to Clapton, knowing how I should disapprove of such an arrangement, she wrote to her brother-in-law to come up to town to accompany her to Clapton, in order to bring Maud home; but a telegram from Maud, saying that she was at Clapton with my consent, stopped them. I would remark that I had only that one interview with my child at Lausanne, and that when I parted with her at the door of her lodgings, the only arrangement then was for her to return home with me.

The following letter written by my dear eldest daughter to her sister at Clapton on the Tuesday will shew how she had been expecting her sister's arrival:—

"CLAPHAM COMMON,
"*Tuesday.*

"Dear Maud,—I am surprised and distressed beyond measure to see that Mr Booth dared say at a meeting last night at Sheffield, that you were at his private house with papa's consent. It is utterly false. You only travelled with Miss Booth because he was unequal to hurrying over the long journey. I heard from him last night that he will be here this evening, and that he did not expect you to arrive in London till Wednesday. If a letter or telegram came to say you were coming earlier, I was to be sure and meet you at the station and bring you *straight* here. I do not know what he will say when he returns to-night. I can only tell you, you are breaking the most loving heart that *ever* beat, by your undutiful, unchristlike conduct. You know how he always was opposed to your going to Clapton, and how he would have prevented it, if you had not made it impossible for him to do so. I did hope the sight of him, broken down with grief, would have touched your heart, if anything could.—Your loving but sadly grieved sister, ANNIE."

In reply to this, Maud wrote a letter to her sister,

which has been destroyed or mislaid; but the following letter, written by her sister in reply, will show how beautifully she endeavoured to second my efforts to reclaim her misguided sister.

CLAPHAM COMMON, *8th February* 1883.

"My Dear Maud,—I think the time has come for me also to write plainly to you. Let me tell you affectionately and solemnly that until you have given up your will to God, and are content to do His will, *whatever* that may be, He cannot guide you.

"I know it is far pleasanter to human nature to be made much of, and to be some one in the eyes of the world, and help in some work that is called great, than to go on quietly and patiently in the daily round of little monotonous duties. But I feel sure that God requires obedience *first*, and that while you are setting your father's wishes at defiance, the Lord Jesus will not accept the work that you have perversely chosen to give Him. He said to some of old, and how true it is to-day: 'Ye say if a man shall say to his father or mother, it is corban, that is to say, a gift (dedicated to God in the Greek), by whatsoever thou mightest be profited by me, he shall be free. And ye suffer him no more to do aught for his father or his mother. Thus have ye made the commandment of God of none effect by your tradition.' Just so, when your Father asks for your love to care and cheer him, you say, 'That is corban, I will not give it you' (fathers do not care to take unwilling gifts from their children). 'Whosoever, therefore, shall break one of these least commandments, and shall teach men so, he shall be called least in the kingdom of heaven.' Yes, Maud, one day *will* reveal every hidden motive, everything that savours of 'self' in men's work, and then you may be surprised to find some old bed-ridden woman humbly doing or suffering for God, placed far above General Booth, with all his fictitious titles and parade of service.

"I know our precious mother did take great interest

in the S.A. meetings; but some of her dearest friends have said to me how certain they are that she would never sanction their present position. Herself a *perfect* daughter and wife, she would never have left her father's or her husband's home as you have done. Let me never hear you again mention her sacred name in connection with the work of the 'Army.' Miss * * * the dearest friend my precious mother had, and the one who most truly understood her inmost soul, thus writes to me this morning:—'Oh that Maud could see her duty, I just keep asking for her an enlightened conscience; and for your father, that the God of all comfort will fit some special consolation to his special need.' Have you, Maudie, ever asked yourself *why* the Lord Jesus was subject to His earthly parents, and in their home living quietly and unostentatiously for thirty years? Surely *He* was more anxious for the souls of sinners than *you* are? Our only guide is God's word. Do you, can you in your right senses, believe that God speaks to you through the lips of any living man, however high and holy you believe him to be? You say, 'It is Jesus I follow, not Mr Booth.' Can you be following Jesus if those you follow are not treading in His steps? Where in the life of that lowly gentle Saviour will you find anything similar to the marching of the S. Army? Oh, Maud, when will you learn to take *His* yoke upon you, who was meek and lowly of heart. When I look at my precious father, one of the most devoted servants that ever laboured for the Master, I think how it must grieve the dear Lord Jesus to see him thus treated by anyone under cover of duty to God, especially by the child to whose hand was entrusted the sweet task of comforting him.

"I send you some verses I wrote for you last month, you will see that in them I gave you credit for the very highest motives. God grant they may be the only ones laid bare when the day comes that the secrets of all hearts are revealed. As to your letter to me, if it were not so very sorrowful, I should only see it in its truly ridiculous light. The idea of a child of your age writing as though free to follow your own chosen way is utterly absurd. I can only hope that it was written for you, and is not your own expression of your own convictions. It is so unlike the little Maudie we loved. I know that the S.A. quite ignores all parental rights, but fortunately the world at large does *not* ignore the God-given authority of a father over his child. Until you are of age you cannot act independently. I do not know dearest papa's address, so have been unable to telegraph to him that you are at Clapton, and that I have not had the chance of bringing you here as he directed.

"May the Lord guide you and shew you His will is ever my earnest prayer.—Your loving sister, ANNIE."

TO MAUD.

"Let every man abide in the same calling in which he was called."
—1 COR. vii. 20.

"How can I serve the Master,
  Who did so much for me?
I will not hide the blessing,
  No, all my light shall see.

"I'll stand in crowded meetings,
  Or in the open street,
And there by earnest pleading
  Bring souls to Jesus' feet.

"I will not mind misgivings,
  Or shrink from public view;
My Saviour bore reviling,
  And I must brave it too.

"Dear are the ties of friendship,
  Dearer the sweet home bliss,
And yet the true disciple
  Will gladly give up this.

"Then do not bid me linger,
  I cannot, dare not stay;
Loud voices call me forward,
  Where God has shewn the way."

. . . . .

SENSATIONAL RELIGION.

"Is it truly the Master
  Who calls? Oh, pause and wait;
And do not force an entrance,
  Where He has closed the gate.

"Oh wait for His sweet whisper,
  Be slow to choose thy way;
The eager voices round thee
  May drown the Master's 'Nay.

"He does call some to action,
  And fits them for the strife;
But He has work for many
  In the sheltered paths of life.

"Would He not have thee comfort
  Some who to Him are dear?
There are little ones to cherish,
  And aching hearts to cheer.

"Beware, lest thou art leaving,
  While further thou dost roam,
The work thy King requireth,
  Forgotten in thy home.

"Beware, for while thus sowing
  The good seed far and wide,
Thy sweet flowers may be drooping,
  Neglected at thy side.

"May be while thou art seeking
  The lost ones for His fold,
Thy Lord may see with sorrow,
  Thy hearth-fires growing cold.

"Ah, none can fill thy corner,
  But empty it must be;
No other hand may finish
  The work planned out for thee.

"See how God's will in Nature
  Has varied each design!
The song-bird has to carol,
  The glow-worm has to shine.

"The palm-tree braves the tempest,
  And springs up strong and tall;
The green moss creeps in silence
  Over the crannied wall.

"The mighty river rushes
   Unchecked both deep and strong;
The streamlet o'er the pebbles
   Tinkles a murmuring song.

"The brilliant poppy tosses
   Her blossoms in the breeze;
The modest scented violet
   Must hide among her leaves.

"May God teach thee thy mission,
   Who else could dare the choice?
But when a summons cometh,
   Make sure it is *His* voice.

"The world is full of echoes
   That mock the Spirit's cry;
The small still voice is silent
   When 'self' is set on high.

"'Tis only empty vessels
   Can hold the perfume sweet
They only can teach others
   Who learn at Jesus' feet.

"Give up thy way to Jesus,
   And let thy heart be still;
Then listen through the silence,
   To hear His loving will.

"He gives to each a service,
   And asks for that alone;
Darling, there lies before thee
   The ministry of home."

Feby. 1883.   A. M. C.

This letter was read at the family breakfast table at Clapton. Maud stated to her sister that it called forth much amusement there.

I must now revert to the evening of my return home. I immediately wrote to Maud the following letter:—

"CLAPHAM COMMON, *8th March* 1883.

"My Dear Child,—I was detained yesterday at Calais through the weather being too rough for the steamboat to leave.

"On arriving here I was grieved to find that you were not here or at Bellevue, and greatly distressed to hear that you have stated I had given my consent to your going to Clapton. I come over to-morrow to fetch you, and you must have your things ready packed to return with me at 11.30.

"Your dear aunt kindly wishes you to come here for a little visit, but as I told you at Lausanne, I will, if you prefer it, arrange to be with you at Norwood, though it is my wish to have you at this dear house with me for a few days first.—Ever your affectionate father,
"SAMUEL CHARLESWORTH."

On the following morning I went over to Clapton with my eldest daughter to fetch Maud. Whilst she was upstairs packing up her things to accompany me, I sat with Mrs Booth. I then told her what Maud had confided to me at Lausanne, and asked her to tell my child, in my presence, that her son was already engaged. She angrily refused, adding, "for aught I can tell there are fifty young girls connected with the Salvation Army feeling towards my son the same as your daughter does." I immediately rose and left the room, and waited in the hall until my daughter was ready to leave.

On my arrival at home on the Thursday evening, my eldest daughter told me that she had received a letter from a friend in Switzerland, stating that I had written a letter to the Genevan newspapers on the previous Tuesday retracting my letter in the *Times*. I told her that she might write and tell her friend that if the Genevan papers contained any such letter purporting to be from me, it was a forgery, for I had written none. The following morning's post solved the mystery, it brought a copy of the newspaper *La Tribune de Genève*, dated Tuesday, 6th March 1883, containing an alleged translation of my private letter to Pasteur Theodore Monod, inserted in that paper even before my letter had reached him.

Of course such a use of my letter was simply carrying out the Army code on the " Use of newspapers," section 9, page 69: " Notices in newspapers of any kind are always of great service; *a capable commanding officer* will therefore take care to be published in them as soon as possible. It is to the interests of the service to be in the columns as often as possible, *no matter in what way.*"

CHAPTER VI.

I BROUGHT home from Clapton, not my once dutiful devoted child, but a young girl who had in heart given herself up to the Army, and who was only waiting to reach the age of eighteen years, in order to carry out fully that heart surrender by solemnly pledging herself to the Army service for life, and binding herself to obey "her General" in everything, though in direct opposition to her father's wishes and commands.

These are the words by which "General Booth" enforces this absolute subjection to himself. See "Army Orders and Regulations," page 2 :—

"As He (God) works by one person upon another, this implies *that He can only do His utmost*, by persons who are in the most perfect and continual subjection to those whom He has chosen to lead them."

This code my daughter accepts as her rule and guide of Christian life and conduct, her "General" being to her in the place not only of her father but also of God. See "Code of Army Doctrines and Discipline."

"*Section 25.—The Bible.*

"*Article* 8. Do not some people set a false value on the Bible?

"Yes, some undervalue it, and in consequence neglect to read, and be governed by its teaching; while others overestimate it, by regarding it as the *only* way in which God speaks to man.

"9. Does God communicate His will to men in any other way than through the written Word?

"Yes; He speaks directly to the heart, by His Spirit, and by *His Spirit also through one man to another.*

"11. Does this promise (John xiv. 16) apply to us, and may we expect its fulfilment?

"Certainly we may. The notion that the fulfilment of this promise was confined to Apostolic times is one of the greatest mistakes ever made. It is therefore wrong and misleading to argue that we have no other way of ascertaining the mind of the Spirit concerning our own salvation, or our duty to our fellows, except through the written Word, and it is one great cause of so much *lame experience* in the knowledge of God, and so much lame effort to extend the kingdom of God. *The living*, active positive agency of God is comparatively shut out of the world, and a *dead* book placed in its stead."

The home where Maud was now staying with me was the home of her mother in childhood, and where in her last illness she had come away from the noise and smoke of Limehouse to enjoy the rest, tranquillity, and pure air of the place of her nativity, under the loving care of her only surviving sister. A merciful arrangement; as in God's providence, after one week of patient endurance of suffering, she was called thence to the home above.

It was in the sacred associations of this home, where Maud had so often formerly passed many happy days, that I hoped to revive her family affections, and to bring her back in love and obedience to me and our other home at Norwood. But no! those four days at Clapton, in the house of the Booths, had effectually done its work; the alienation was complete, the separation unavoidable; she would hardly speak to her sister and her kind devoted aunt. She stayed up in her own bed-room, and seemed not to care for their society. One day she received a telegram from Miss Booth, stating that she was coming down to see her. I sent a message back forbidding her to come, nevertheless she came, bringing a Mrs Onslow with her; and as they were shown into the drawing-room before we knew of their arrival, my relative and I felt that we could not in Christian courtesy turn them out of the house. Painful and unsatisfactory in the extreme was the interview. With Maud, of course, it had its effect in strengthening her feelings and resolve.

On Monday the 12th a great meeting of the Salvation Army was to be held, at which Miss Booth was to give an account of the persecutions in Switzerland. Late on the previous Saturday evening the solicitor of "General Booth" came down to me at Clapham to make a special request that Maud might be allowed to attend, but I had already decided that I would take her there, as I felt it essential to be present in order to contradict any incorrect statements which might be made as to the part I had taken with reference to my daughter. For that object only I went there.

Previous to the meeting I saw the "General" in his council chamber, crowded with staff officers and friends of the Army. It was difficult to realise that the war-like, authoritative, rudely out-spoken man, with exuberant beard and moustache, was the gentle courteous man of shaven face and humble attire who eight years before had come to me in my church vestry to ask for the use of one of my schoolrooms. Between whiles we had never met or spoken together. Then he was the originator and leader of a truly apostolic work, the humble but most useful "Christian Mission," now he was the autocratic General and Commander-in-Chief of the Salvation Army. As a father I pleaded and remonstrated with him earnestly on behalf of my child, but I soon found that the stern General bent on the conquest of the world had no room in his breast for the feelings of a father or the charity of a Christian. The crowded meeting was waiting for the great man. I was soon cut short by the following declaration, which I afterwards wrote down in pencil, though its words were burnt into my memory: "Your daughter is ours, and she will be ours for life; you may force her to go home and break her heart, and send her to an early grave, but she will be ours to death."

I and Maud sat quietly by ourselves in a side gallery throughout the day's meetings, nevertheless the reporters were instructed to take down our names which appeared in the newspaper reports as though we had been on the platform officially attending the meeting.

It is now my painful and somewhat difficult task to explain why and how, after my confidence in Miss Booth was gone, I should again commit my daughter to her charge on her return to Switzerland.

After the death of my wife, when I resigned the parish of Limehouse, I contemplated taking some small ministerial charge, where I and my two unmarried daughters might find a tranquil home, and engage in quiet parochial work. Maud's adhesion to the Salvation Army put a stop to this plan, rendering my future movements so uncertain and perplexing. I therefore devoted myself to assisting gratuitously clerical relatives and friends, who through illness or other emergency needed temporary help.

But here again Maud's presence at home was a great hinderance. I was obliged often to be absent from home, from Saturday to Monday, and sometimes to be away for weeks together. I could not take her with me, I could not leave her at home. She had altogether ceased to feel any interest in our church services, and in our week-day home occupations and engagements. The presence of her eldest sister at home was distasteful to her. My once bright, happy, and dutiful child was gone, so entire a change had come over her since that untoward visit to the Booth family. One only object seemed now to fill her mind and heart—the Salvation Army and its adherents; all other interests and duties had lost their hold upon her regard. Home was a dull place to her, and her presence had become a cloud there. But a stronger reason forced me to a decision as to the future. I saw with alarm that her health was failing, and that morbid excitement and restlessness of mind foreboded a serious form of illness. Absence of any occupation of interest in the day and sleepless nights made life a burden to her. In our conversations together as to our future arrangements, I found that nothing would satisfy her but Army service. The Booths still kept up their paramount influence by letters; the *War Cry* with its exciting details was ever in her hand or pocket. I had requested Miss Booth not to come to our house, but one morning a letter or telegram arrived to say she was coming. I could only prevent her by going up to the Head-Quarters in Queen Victoria Street, where I found a cab at the door waiting to take her to the station. This attempt of Miss Booth again to force herself on our home privacy brought matters to a crisis. I felt that I could no longer bear my child at home. To give her up to the Army in London was simply to wreck her life, by throwing her constantly in the way of a man who had drawn forth her affections as a child of sixteen, but who was then engaged to be married to another. Now at seventeen years of age a continuance of that feeling would be, under the circumstances, most harmful to her character and happiness. Will any parent who can enter into the difficulties of such a position for a father, blame me that I turned my thoughts even to Miss Booth and her work in Switzerland as a loophole of escape, or rather as a less evil of two dangers?

The following correspondence will best explain how I endeavoured to carry out this seemingly unavoidable arrangement.

"CLAPHAM COMMON, 15*th March* 1883.

"Dear Miss Booth,—My future course of action with regard to my dear child Maud is to me, as you must suppose, a subject of intense anxiety. Her remaining at home with me is, I fear, now out of the question. She is so changed. Her exposure on the streets of Paris selling the *En Avant*, and the rough exciting scenes she passed through in Switzerland, with other kindred influences, have altered her character mournfully. The question now is whether she be placed by me under the care of others until she reaches twenty-one years of age, without permission to have any further communication with the Salvation Army, or whether I again run the risk of allowing her in a modified and controlled form to engage in your work. In my painful interview with your father on Monday at Exeter Hall, he said, 'Your daughter is ours, ours so long as she lives; you may force her to be at home with you, and break her heart or bring her to an early grave, but she will be ours until death.' That word 'ours' is terribly true; my child is lost to me, alienated from the Church of her parents, from the loved home of her childhood, from relatives and friends, and from all the associations and interests of her previous life. It is a bitter trial. I could give her up to the Lord and His service in any form, but I do not now recognise Christ in the Salvation Army, or His work in their work.

"This leads me to the all important subject of your doctrines and teaching. I read over with Colonel Clibborn portions of a book entitled, I think, 'Catechism or Orders and Discipline of the Salvation Army.' That book I find I can now buy, so I shall obtain it and study it. But there is another important book which I have not seen and know not how to obtain. It is in six parts, being Orders and Regulations for the Salvation Army. I have part one, in which reference is made to the other parts, and those I am anxious to see, as so intimately affecting my dear child, if she is allowed to join the Army.

"Next to the question of doctrine is the all important one of her happiness and future welfare. God knows how dear they are to me. I have often mentioned to members of your family how I dread the excitement of your meetings and system of work upon a mind so sensitive, impulsive, and inexperienced. I also mentioned to you another very private reason why Clapton and London are such undesirable spheres of action for her. If she is allowed to continue in any way connected with the Army, it must be for these reasons abroad, and not in England. Many other Christian workers in England and abroad have written to me proposing to take her to be associated with them, but the question is her happiness and her inclinations, so far as I can yield to them. There have been so many unfair misrepresentations appearing in the public journals that I prefer that our communications should be in writing, and not in conversation. My painful interviews with your mother and father cause me to shrink from exposing myself to any further scenes of that nature. Oh, that the Lord may guide and direct us all through this tangled web of opposing thoughts and feelings and purposes.—Believe me to be, dear Miss Booth, yours very faithfully, "SAMUEL CHARLESWORTH."

20th March 1883.

"Dear Miss Booth,—Your not having replied to my letter of the 15th instant places me in much perplexity. Maud tells me you leave for Paris early the day after to-morrow. She is most anxious to go with you, because she thinks she can be a comfort to you in travelling. The journey to and from Switzerland has so tried me, I could not venture on another foreign journey.

"Since Maud has been with me here I have had long anxious talks with her. To me she is the same loving child as ever, but I see too clearly that her heart is no longer in her home, that her thoughts, interests, and deepest affections are with your family and the Salvation Army. Your father's words to me—'Your daughter is ours, and will be ours so long as she lives'—are indeed true.

"Not hearing from you, but being obliged this morning to come to a decision, I have had a final talk with Maud, and she has, as her own deliberate choice, the outcome of her own desire, though opposed to my wishes and my judgment, decided to return to Paris with you. Your father said, 'I might force her to be at home with me and break her heart, and bring her to an early grave.' I will not so force her or even seek to constrain her. I have told her all I feel, but her happiness and spiritual welfare are too dear to me to compel her to take a course that may endanger either.

"I am sure that the services and worship of my own Church will not satisfy her cravings after more sensational and exciting modes of worship. Also, I am sure that she will never settle down to a routine of quiet study and home occupation, and that her continuance at home will not be for her own comfort or the comfort of myself and my dear eldest daughter. Therefore, and for these considerations alone, I allow her to act upon her decision and to return with you.

"I will allow her £100 per annum, but that sum must cover all her expenses, as it is not in my power to give her more. I paid you £25 in Paris in advance, and I will now give her £50 to take with her to make up the arrears, and to continue on her payments to you, but I do not wish these amounts to appear in the Salvation Army accounts. I must stipulate that, until she is eighteen years of age, she is only with you as a young friend and guest, and not to be officially connected with the Army.

"As I understand that many marriages have resulted from the intercourse of young people in their fellowship together in the Army, I wish it to be distinctly known and understood that under no circumstances will I consent to Maud's marriage under the age of twenty-one years.

"If you will write me word by what train you start on Thursday, I will bring Maud to the station to meet you.—Believe me to be yours very sincerely,

"SAMUEL CHARLESWORTH."

The following is Miss Booth's reply, or rather acknowledgment of my two previous letters:—

"*23rd March.*

"Dear Mr Charlesworth,—Saturday to Wednesday I was away from home, holding meetings in different towns. Your letter arrived at Clapton, and was forwarded after me. I am sorry for the delay.

"You are entirely wrong in writing as if we wished to take your daughter away from your home to a foreign land away from your influence. Nothing of the kind. I not only do not wish so to take her, but I will not do so, unless you can see your way to send her precisely as you left her in Paris—for *Christ's sake!* I utterly repudiate the insinuation of some secondary motive on our part; and as long as you seek to connect any such suspicion with your daughter's presence with me, so long please understand that I utterly refuse to have her, much as I value her help, and shall feel separation from her, and much as I shall deplore its effect on the work itself.—Yours faithfully, "CATHERINE BOOTH."

"*23rd March* 1883.

"Dear Miss Booth,—My letter was written to you on the 15th inst. Surely on such an important subject as a father entirely giving up his child to strangers, to be united with them probably for life in a foreign land, it was due to me that thirty minutes should be set aside out of your important engagements to reply to my letter.

"You seemed greatly pained at the stipulation which I put into my letter with the desire to guard against my dear child falling into the danger of an early engagement and premature marriage; but surely, when she is leaving my roof, and my watchful care, and guidance, and counsel, to live among strangers in a foreign land, such a caution on my part for her sake is justifiable.

"You and your family seem to me entirely to overlook the most trying and sorrowful circumstances of my position as a father.

"You and they are desiring to engross her as a member of the Salvation Army in a way that involves her leaving me, her home, her relatives, and all present associations at the early age of seventeen years. Surely there is some consideration due to a father's feelings when he is asked to make such a sacrifice, especially when the work in which my daughter is to engage is not work of which in its principles and proceedings I can approve. She feels it under your and their guidance and influence to be the Lord's call to her to enter His service, therefore I yield her up, knowing the sincerity and purity of her motives; and as I believe the Continent is a less objectionable sphere than England for her to be so engaged, I give my consent to her accompanying you, to be united with you in your work as a young friend, hoping that the Lord may bless her in her heart's devotion to his service. If you will take charge of her under these circumstances, I will bring her to Cannon Street Station to meet you to-morrow; but, remember, it must not be said or thought that I have sought or desired that my child should leave me or her home. I allow it, because I feel it may be for her happiness and peace of mind, but very sorrowfully. Believe me to be, yours very faithfully,

"SAMUEL CHARLESWORTH."

"114 CLAPTON COMMON,
"LONDON, E., 24*th March* 1883.

"Dear Mr Charlesworth,—You are entirely mistaken in supposing I wish you to say anything beyond what you mean. All I ask is that Maud's coming with me shall not be accompanied with unworthy insinuations which would lead me to expect some future attack in the press, such as we have had to suffer in the past.

"I quite appreciate the difficulty of your position, but you must remember that mine is not less unpleasant. I receive along with yours a letter from your daughter telling me she feels her body will not endure the strain for six months. But for the *distress* that her sad letter causes me I should not be inclined to say any more at present, but in the hope of relieving you both from all this distress and anxiety which makes you write so differently to what you did formerly. I enclose copy of a letter as nearly as possible in *your own words*, which you will surely sign. I but *too keenly* realize what you say about Maud's mind. This is a matter of conscience with her, and I believe if you allow her to follow her convictions you will never have reason to regret it throughout eternity.

"I do hope there will be no more misunderstanding, and that I with dearest Maud will be able to work for our blessed Lord in that perfect peace which is so necessary in this great fight between right and wrong. Yours, following Jesus, "CATHERINE BOOTH."

"*29th March* 1883.

"Dear Miss Booth,—I was so grieved on finding from your telegram to Maud on Tuesday that you were too ill to return to Paris on that day, and my dear child was in the night so greatly distressed with an overwhelming feeling that by her telegram to you on Monday she had withdrawn herself from the Lord's call and work, a distress which caused us both sleepless nights, that on Wednesday morning by our first post after breakfast I wrote a line to you saying that if you had not left for Paris on that day she should return with you on Thursday. You had left, and, therefore, my chief object in wishing her to be a comfort to you on your journey was defeated. I have now time once again to write to you, and I am anxious to say that I doubt you do not fully feel or make allowance for the gravity of my position. As to my feelings and wishes as a father in desiring to retain Maud a little longer in her home, those I have entirely given up as a stern necessity for what I feel to be her happiness and peace of mind in following what she considers to be the Lord's call and guidance. I cannot set up my wishes as a parent in opposition to that which may affect her spiritual well-being. But there is another light in which I have to regard this perplexed, difficult subject springing out of a reason which has throughout most weighed with me.

"As a clergyman of the Church of England of nearly thirty years' standing in a prominent position, I have the responsibility of my example and influence, whatever they may be or however they may act upon others. As it is well known, and has been for many years, how strongly I feel many grave objections to the principles and proceedings of the Salvation Army, I cannot consistently or honestly allow it to be supposed that my child returns under your care by my desire and at my voluntary request. You on your part, as shewn by your late correspondence on this subject, evidently seek to throw upon me that responsibility in full, declining to have her except on that understanding. You assume that I should make use of her return to you, if you be not so guarded, as a further ground of reflection on the Salvation Army. But ought it to be supposed that after so giving back my child to you, I should ever say a word condemnatory of you or the Army because of her return. You know well that my letter to the *Times* was caused solely and entirely by the publication of my child's private letter to your father. But for that sorrowful exposure I should never have breathed one syllable of my feelings towards the Army. It was not the fact of my felt responsibility before referred to which drew forth my letter; other things have since occurred which have pained me even more, but for your sake and the sake of the work in which you are engaged, I have not made them public. If your father had replied to my first letter in a courteous candid manner I should have never written the second, or a word further than the first. Your late correspondence leads me with greater reason to infer that my consent to Maud's return to Paris and Switzerland would be publicly announced in like words to those spoken by your father at Sheffield, and to those erroneously stated to have been spoken by you at Exeter Hall, completely compromising my position and character.

"Such is the trying nature of my present position, overwhelmed as I am with letters on the subject, both from the Continent and all parts of England. On me must rest the responsibility of Maud's return, unless it be clearly understood why and how she returns.

"Believe me to be, yours very truly,
"SAMUEL CHARLESWORTH."

3 AVENUE LAUMIERE, RUE D' ALLEMAGNE,
PARIS, 30*th March* 1883.

"Dear Mr Charlesworth,—My late correspondence has been necessarily of a business character, as your letters seemed to require. I had far rather it had been otherwise. Your conditions need not have been written so emphatically; if you had only expressed them it would have been quite sufficient.

"I do not think I overlook your position as a father, nor am I blind to the anxiety you must feel in deciding on so important a matter. I fully sympathise with you, yet you give her to the Lord, not to me. I only wish to guard against it being said (as it *has* been said) that Maud is with me without your consent and *against your wish*, and this is chiefly important as it touches the 'work' which is dearer to me than all else.

"You know that I shall look after Maud's highest interest, and watch over her as one of my own sisters. She is *very* dear to me, not only for her own sake, but for the help she has been to me in this great struggle.

"I cannot help the conviction that the Lord has chosen your child, and 'hath need' of her, and I believe He will use her mightily for His glory, and that you will have great cause to rejoice over her.

"As to the letters you receive from abroad, what have people on the Continent to do with you or me or Maud in this matter? If we have confidence in one another, what more is needed? You and Maud are influenced by widely different motives from those which actuate outsiders.

"I will write you freely about your dear child; and I need not add that I will take every precaution to prevent Maud's name being again subject to the publicity which has been so painful both to you and to me. If you will wire the train you come by we will meet you.

"Excuse this hurried letter. I am suffering from my back.—Believe me, yours ever following hard after my Master, "CATHERINE BOOTH."

"*31st March* 1883.

"Dear Miss Booth,—Only telegrams have reached us to indicate your arrangements. The experience and added knowledge of each day confirm and deepen sorrowfully my regret that my daughter, Maud, should of her own deliberate choice leave the home of her parent and cast aside all its once treasured associations and interests, to connect herself with a religious system in which I can feel no sympathy, but of which in its principles and proceedings as developed in London I greatly disapprove. Nevertheless, as it is her firm conviction that in her work with the Salvation Army she has the Lord's call and guidance, I fear to withstand her convictions, because I see how deeply rooted they are, and I fear that to withdraw her from the Salvation Army worship and work might not only endanger her health of mind and body, but what I dread far more, her spiritual life. She has become so dependent upon the excitement and material adjuncts of the Army for her channels of devotion and spiritual nourishment, that now to break her away from those aids might cause a reaction and lead to apathy or some other extreme. An important business engagement detains me in London until Monday, the 9th April, but after that day I can bring her to you in Switzerland, only I must travel by short stages, and may have to rest on the journey a day or two.

"Will you in the meantime send me a full copy of my letter mentioning the conditions on which she returns to the Army work on the Continent. I wrote that letter late at night in my bed-room, whilst your messenger waited for it, and my memory fails to recall correctly the contents. Of course I should never think of making public that or any other letter passing between us, unless it became necessary to contradict any future statement made as to my desiring to hand over my child to the Salvation Army. No one abhors more than I do the resort to newspaper controversy.

"Again I ask, as I asked through my daughter when I before came to Lausanne, that we may not meet. All the circumstances attending our interviews are so intensely painful to me, that I would rather not have any interview with you or Colonel Clibborn, but simply leave my child and hasten away from a land so fraught with the bitterest memories to me as a father. Believe me to be, yours very faithfully,
"SAMUEL CHARLESWORTH."

With a sorrowful heart I again crossed the Channel with my poor child, with the intention of taking her to Switzerland; but in Paris my health broke down entirely. I had a serious illness, and was obliged to return home as soon as I could travel. I sent Maud on to Switzerland under the care of a young woman going to Miss Booth.

Shortly after Maud's return to Switzerland, paragraphs appeared from time to time in many London and country newspapers, reporting her engagement and intended marriage to one of "General" Booth's sons, with painful comments on the subject. I wrote to several of the editors, and endeavoured to find out the origin of this rumour. I traced it up to a journal in which short biographical notices of the Booth family had appeared, but I could obtain no further clue or information. I then wrote the following letter to Miss Booth:

"*23rd April* 1883.

"Dear Miss Booth,—I cannot authorise you to publish in any form that my daughter has returned to work with the Salvation Army with my consent. She has returned to Switzerland with my concurrence, but against my wish. If the one be stated publicly, the other must appear, or I shall cause it to appear. I have this morning been informed that there is again a mutilated version of my letter to the British Ambassador at Berne, inserted in some reply of the Salvation Army to a pamphlet by the Countess de Gasparin. This is wrong. Also I have seen a statement in some of the London journals that my daughter is about to be married to one of General Booth's sons. I hope this wicked falsehood, so injurious both to her, poor child, and to the cause of the Army, has not emanated from any member of your family. I told Colonel Clibborn in my last letter to him, that I must decline signing any document of appeal in any form. If you have occasion to send my daughter home, pray do not do as you propose, send her by one of your girls. Write me word of your desire, and I will come and fetch her myself at once, or if unable, send a messenger for her. Believe me to be, yours faithfully,

"SAMUEL CHARLESWORTH."

I received no reply whatever to this letter.

The conflicts between the Salvation Army soldiers and the Swiss police authorities were soon renewed, not now in the Canton of Geneva, whence my child had been expelled, but in the Cantons of Neuchatel and Berne. Maud, however, did not take any very prominent part in them, and was only occasionally referred to in the newspaper reports as the companion of Miss Booth. But in the month of September following her return to Switzerland, she accompanied Miss Booth into the Canton of Geneva to attend the funeral of a Salvationist; they were both arrested by the police, and conveyed to the frontier of the Canton, and then discharged. My daughter by entering the Canton from which she had been already expelled had rendered herself liable to a long term of imprisonment. But the authorities dealt very generously and courteously with her, only sending her with an escort to the frontier. Miss Booth incurred no such penalty, as she was only interdicted from entering the Canton to hold meetings, &c., and had not been previously expelled. On this occasion I wrote to my daughter the following letter:—

"*18th September* 1883.

"My Dear Maud,—I am surprised and grieved at not hearing from you to acknowledge the cheque for £25 which I sent to you twelve days since, and to return to me the paper, either signed or unsigned, which I enclosed to you three weeks ago, and for the return of which I have twice written. Also I am most distressed that Miss Booth has allowed you again to be disgraced by being arrested by the Geneva police. Having been expelled from the Canton of Geneva you had no right to go there under any circumstances or for any cause. If Miss Booth chose to infringe the law or rules of the Canton by returning there, she ought not to have allowed you to do so. I now therefore revoke the exercise of choice which I unhappily gave you, and I desire that you do not join the Army in any form, as I cannot trust you or Miss Booth as to what impropriety you may commit. I will not have any child of mine, whilst she is under my control, and I am responsible for her actions, thus exposing herself to insult and imprisonment, and causing her name to be bandied about in the public journals. There is no true religion in a system which leads to such a course of action, and you shall not be associated with those who drag you into it. I am, your affectionate father, "SAMUEL CHARLESWORTH."

In consequence of this letter Miss Booth sent Maud away from Switzerland to Paris. I believe she travelled alone unprotected. In France she concealed her place of residence from me, so that I could not go and bring her home, not knowing where to find her.

Reports still appearing in the papers about her

intended marriage, I wrote the following letter to Mr Booth:—

"The Rev. William Booth,
  "Army Head-Quarters,
    "101 Queen Victoria Street, E.C.

"Sir,—During the past six months numerous statements have appeared in London journals to the effect that my young daughter, Maud Charlesworth, was about to marry one of your sons. As I have no personal knowledge whatever of your sons, and as my daughter has never with my consent had any communication or intercourse with them, I wrote to several of the principal papers containing these rumours, denying their truth. I also wrote to Miss Booth, under whose care my child then was, on the subject, but she has taken no notice whatever of my letter of inquiry; in fact, she has not once written to me since I so reluctantly, in April last, allowed my poor child to return to her custody.

"As I was a year since informed on undoubted authority that the son in question was engaged to a young lady connected with the 'Army,' I should have been thankful if a contradiction to these, to me, most painful reports, had also emanated from 'head-quarters,' seeing that the 'General-in-Chief' exercises such absolute control over the engagements and marriages of his 'Officers.'

"But perhaps, sir, to allay my anxiety, lest my young daughter should be drawn into a marriage, which I consider would wreck her life, you will favour me with a report from 'head-quarters,' whether the 'General-in-Chief' has in this instance approved and given his consent to any such engagement.

"I wish to add that in my interviews and correspondence with my poor child since her association with the 'Army,' I have with trembling noticed such a tendency to unnatural morbid excitement, almost bordering on derangement, that I feel her case requires peculiar gentleness, delicacy, and discretion in any dealings with her.

"I wrote to your daughters and Mrs Booth, anxiously cautioning them on this subject; but as I was told my letters occasioned you much amusement, and called forth facetious comments, I hesitate again to express more fully my fears.

"I have ascertained that on the 21st February last a telegram was sent from 'Head-quarters' to my daughter, then in Switzerland with Miss Booth, commencing 'sightless father,' and ending 'adoring.' May I ask if that telegram was penned by one of your sons, and may I request the favour of being furnished with a copy of the reply immediately telegraphed by her. I must beg to have a written answer, as I still continue to decline to have any personal interview with any one connected with the Army. I am, sir, yours faithfully,
"SAMUEL CHARLESWORTH.

"BEAUCHAMP ROAD, NORWOOD,
    3rd October 1883."

To this letter I received the following insolent reply. I write insolent, having regard to its being written to an aged clergyman and father by a young man, who, though called a Colonel and Chief of Staff, was in reality but one of many clerks employed by William Booth to carry on the machinery of his gigantic religious operations. It will be observed that the letter ignores entirely my question about the marriage rumours. I am therefore entitled to infer that these reports did emanate from head-quarters, and were, in fact, intended to pioneer the way, in Army newspaper fashion, for my consent to her marriage, which was so soon after sought to be wrung from me.

"HEADQUARTERS OF THE SALVATION ARMY,
    101 QUEEN VICTORIA STREET, LONDON, E.C.,
        4th October 1883.

"Rev. S. Charlesworth.

"Sir,—My father, who had to leave town to-day, charged me to say in reply to yours simply that, being quite weary of your extraordinary conduct, and of the strange return you have so long made for the kindness shown your daughter, by your own admission, ever since you requested last Easter that she should be allowed once more to be with Miss Booth, he has already felt compelled to tell her that, if she is to remain with Miss Booth, who has so many other more cares than she is able to endure, she must see you, and put a stop for ever to all these inexcusable attacks upon people who have never given you any cause for them.

"No doubt when she sees you, she will give you the explanation of the code telegram to which you refer, and which was addressed by me to her at the time of your last letters to the *Times;* and although you do not name the source from which you obtained your information, I may add that the words which you quote were cyphers, the real meaning of which was widely different from the one suggested by your letter.—Yours faithfully,

"W. Bramwell Booth."

CHAPTER VII.

I FELT very grateful to the Swiss authorities for the leniency shown to my misguided child. She might have been imprisoned at Geneva for a long period, and I could not have urged a word in her behalf, except pleading her youth, and that she was led into those irregularities by the indiscretion of those who had the charge of her. I knew what offence her letter in the *Times* had given to the authorities, and therefore felt the more thankful that she was free. During the whole of those unwise conflicts with the Swiss authorities and police I had been strongly urged by the Army people to appeal against the decision of the authorities, and to bring myself into the mêlèe, but I indignantly refused. From the first I felt that the Salvationists were altogether in the wrong, and though my daughter was the victim of their indiscretion I could neither justify nor palliate her conduct. As to its being persecution, the idea was absurd. The Salvationists were aiming throughout at notoriety. They were acting on the Code of Orders and Regulations by getting themselves "noticed in the newspapers as often as possible, no matter in what way." They courted, nay they provoked persecution, as they called it, because the cause throve upon it, it brought funds into the Army exchequer. It made them notorious as heroes and heroines. As to the persecutions, at least so far as the English sufferers were concerned, being a subject of concern or apprehension it was more often one of merriment and rejoicing. It was indeed different as to the poor Swiss converts who had been dragged into the affray; they received treatment from which the more favoured English on account of their nationality and privileged position were exempt. When Miss Booth was accommodated for a few days in her comfortable apartments in the Castle at Neuchatel the repose and quiet must have been to her most refreshing and tranquillising. To call that either persecution or even imprisonment is truly a misnomer.

When I read of the monster prayer meeting convened at Exeter Hall, first for deliverance of the captives, then for thanksgiving for their deliverance, I felt shocked beyond expression that so holy a privilege and duty as prayer and praise should be thus travestied. Of course to the Army at home the collections at both these meetings mitigated in some measure the rigour of the trial. £10,000 was no small compensation for such persecutions. I do not write these words lightly, but in sober and sorrowful earnestness; for I have unhappily been behind the scenes; and as my daughter has been one of the persecuted, I have a right to bear my testimony. Certainly in her case she drew much fun out of her tribulation; and I question whether her comrades did not shed more tears in laughter than in sorrow at her sufferings. Her letter of banter in the *Times* showed the dread with which she regarded her persecutors.

For more than twelve months past the General has been sending my child all over the United Kingdom as the Swiss heroine to recount all the sufferings of herself and her persecuted comrades. She has attended more than 200 crowded meetings, admission 1s., 6d., and 3d. Some thousands of pounds must thus have rolled into the Army exchequer. Even in this, my native town of Ipswich, almost the first placard which attracted my attention was a bill announcing her intended advent to recount her experiences in Switzerland; and I hear that the meetings were a great success to overflowing. We know from the *War Cry* how the temperature of barrack meetings provokes growth in expression and delineation; and I doubt not the facts on which the Swiss persecutions were founded grew greatly in dimensions under the atmospheric heat of those many crowded meetings. But it is intensely mournful when religion is thus made the vehicle for money getting. In all the Army meetings the money box, and the penitent form, collections, and conversions vie with each other in importance. I fear the poor young captains in the provinces have hard work to obtain the funds which they are expected to raise. The "General" in his Book of Orders and Regulations gives most ample instructions for collecting these offerings. Sections 1 and 5 on this subject are a remarkable compendium of the way to get the money from the poor.

"Page 63, article 14. From the first the commanding officer must explain to his men how we hate the penny-a-week system, and by showing a good example himself, he will ensure a handsome custom of weekly offerings.

"Article 16. It is a ruinous system to encourage the idea of getting help from rich people and allowing the poor to be as little benevolent as possible."

After remaining some days in Paris or the neighbourhood, my daughter received a telegram from head-quarters to return to England; an order resulting, I believe, from the letter I wrote on the 3rd October. After staying a short time at the Booths' house, she went down to see her married sister in Hertfordshire. I went to see her there after a separation of six months. In the presence of her sister and her sister's husband, a clergyman, I made an earnest appeal to her to go home with me. She peremptorily refused, saying that if I forced her to go home she would not stay. On my asking whether her "General's" orders and wishes were more binding on her than mine, she said they were. Feeling it impossible to move her, I wrote a letter to Mr Booth, which she read over and signed in testimony of its correctness. The following is a copy :—

"BEAUCHAMP ROAD, NORWOOD, S.E.,
"*8th October* 1883.

"Dear Sir,—I have been summoned down to * * *, to the house of my married daughter Mrs * * *, to see my dear child Maud. I find her looking very ill, with a painful abstractedness and wildness of expression that distresses and alarms me greatly. After a long talk with her, I find her determined in her desire to unite with the Salvation Army. She does not wish to go home with me, and says that if taken there, she cannot and will not remain. I dare not require her return home or thwart her present wishes. I must simply leave her the choice to follow her own inclinations; she is now eighteen years of age.

"But I must make two stipulations,—that she does not until of legal age marry without my consent; and that she does not involve herself in any breach of the law in any country where she may be residing.

"Having come to this decision, I need hardly say that I shall abstain from any further newspaper or public comment upon her connection with the Army, unless any statement emanating from the Army should be made that she has joined it by my wish or with my consent, or unless there be any infraction of the terms made or implied in this letter.—I am, dear sir, yours very faithfully, "SAMUEL CHARLESWORTH."

"This letter has been read over to me by my father.
"MAUD E. CHARLESWORTH."

Afterwards she returned to the house at Clapton, and I went home to Norwood, feeling all further effort to regain her was useless, that henceforth I must regard her as entirely lost to me and her family.

CHAPTER VIII.

I NOW come to the most lamentable and the most painful part of this mournful narrative. Two days after I had written the foregoing letter in the last chapter, I was staying at Clapham, when I received a telegram from my servant at my house at Norwood, saying that Maud had come home. I went there as quickly as possible. She met me at the door with a bright smile, and kissed me fondly, saying, "Oh dear papa, I am come home to stay with you." I could hardly believe it true. We had tea pleasantly together as in olden times, excepting that her eldest sister was away at Clapham. After tea she played on the piano, and for an hour sang to me our favourite hymns; she then asked me to have a game of chess, as was often our evening custom, and afterwards family prayers closed our happy evening. I dared not ask any questions, lest the joyous spell should be broken. Noticing how pale she looked, I proposed that on the morrow we should go off for a fortnight to one of our favourite seaside places of resort in former days. She gladly assented, saying it would do her good. I retired to rest that night with a heart most grateful to God for the restoration of my long-lost child. For joy I slept little. I concluded that my letter to Mr Booth had at length aroused him and his wife to a sense of the cruel wrong they were inflicting upon me, by harbouring my child in their house, and sanctioning her in her desertion of her father and her home, and that they had counselled her to return to me. I loved her with an intense devotion, and her mother's death had made her presence in my home the more needful and dear to me. In the morning she came down to breakfast with all her former bright and loving manner. After breakfast we had our usual Bible reading and prayer together. When she rose from her knees, she said, "I have a letter from my General for you." I trembled as I took the letter, it seemed at once to bring a dark shadow over us.

The following is a verbatim copy :—

"*Private and Confidential.*]

"101 QUEEN VICTORIA STREET,
"LONDON, E.C., *Oct.* 10*th*, 1883.

" Rev. S. Charlesworth.

" Dear Sir,—I have your letter of the 8th instant, and observe that you now give your consent to your daughter joining the Army as an officer.

" I also note the conditions you append to your consent, and think them reasonable.

" But I already discern the possibility of circumstances arising, of which I hasten to apprise you. You are aware, and have been, I know for some time, of the strong affection your daughter entertains for my son Ballington. I find that he has been made aware of this, and I can see how probable it is that an engagement may be desired between them, and according to the understanding between us, I inform you of this.

" The matter is not in *any way of my seeking*, and I cannot hear of it without your knowledge, and it would be exceedingly unpleasant to me either now or at any future time without your full consent.

" You must judge therefore what course it is wisest and best in the interests of your daughter to take. If you think proper to do so, and can dissuade your daughter from any further thoughts of the matter, I will co-operate with you in any reasonable arrangements that can be made.

" I think it best to send Maude with this, in order that there may be some decided course agreed to.

" Much as I love your dear daughter, and value her co-operation, and strongly as I believe in her *disin-*

terested love for the Army, I cannot allow myself to be laid open to any further misinterpretations of purpose and action with respect to her relation to this enterprise.—Believe me, dear sir, to be yours faithfully,

"WILLIAM BOOTH."

After reading this shocking letter, I turned to my daughter and said, "My dear child, do you know how this letter compromises you; what a false position it places you in?" An expression of anger passed over her face, the look of love was entirely gone, she said passionately, "You do not understand my General, and you never will."

I must draw a veil over the remainder of that sorrowful day—the darkest, the saddest day of my long life. The following letters give a faint glimpse of its misery to me.

"BEAUCHAMP ROAD, NORWOOD, S.E.,
"12*th October* 1883.

"To the Rev. William Booth.

"Sir,—In reply to your letter given to me by my daughter this morning, I beg to say that I have never given my consent to her joining the Army. But inasmuch as she has told me that she can only be happy in working for Christ in the Army, and as she has made me fear that her spiritual life might be injured if she were hindered from joining the Army, I have, now that she is eighteen years of age, left her free to follow her own choice.

"As I have told you and other members of your family often before, I have been watching over my poor child with intense anxiety. I have seen symptoms in her of unnatural excitement and morbid states of feeling, which have made me tremble for her sanity. To-day she has twice told me that she should destroy herself, and she is now lying in bed in a state of distraction.

"I have been all and done all to that dear child, the most loving, devoted, tender father could do or be, but now I am hopeless—I am helpless.

"No one but God knows how I loved that child—how inexpressibly dear she has been to me. Two years ago she was the most loving, gentle, sweetest, and docile of children to me—the sunbeam of my home, the joy of my life. Now she is utterly changed, entirely alienated from the home and church of her youth, and from all relatives, associations, and interests connected with both. Oh! William Booth, I have been for more than thirty years a minister of the Gospel, and through a long life of sixty-six years I have, I hope, ever as a Christian minister and a gentleman gained the love and esteem of those I have been associated with. And now I call the God of heaven to witness that you and your family and your system have brought upon my heart its bitterest trial, and upon my life its darkest shadows.

"May the just God requite you. I leave myself and my cruel wrong in His hands.

"My daughter, by her own choice, returns to your house to-morrow. I feel it is either that or a lunatic asylum. Her bewildered mind can bear the strain no longer; and as you may save her from insanity, surely you will not add to my cup of misery by avoiding the only course that seems to be open to avert it. The time was when I could have rescued my child from the impending evil; but now my only course is submission, and with a broken heart and a withered life I part with her for ever.

"As to the other part of your letter with reference to her marriage to your son, I know nothing of him. I have never spoken to him; she surely has only seen him in religious meetings. No! I will not add this risk to my poor child's wrecked life.—I am, sir, your obedient servant, "SAMUEL CHARLESWORTH."

"BEAUCHAMP ROAD, NORWOOD, S.E.,
13th October 1883.

"Mrs Booth,—My poor child is in a most critical state of health both mind and body. At Little Amwell and here she has been like one deranged.

"Yesterday she locked herself up in her bed-room, and refused to see our family medical man or to take any medicine. She states that you only can understand the nature of her illness, and have arranged to take her to an eminent doctor. Therefore I have no course left open but to send her back to you. She twice yesterday threatened to destroy herself, and the medical man advised that she should be put under restraint. This must be done unless the symptons abate. My servants are very thoughtful, but I cannot leave the house with her in it.

"Two years ago this dear child was one of the brightest, sweetest, and most loving and gentle of children, the sunbeam of my home, the joy of my heart, now she is a wreck.

"May God be merciful unto her and restore her.—I am, yours obediently, "SAMUEL CHARLESWORTH."

I learned from my poor child that she had arranged, so soon as she had obtained my consent to her engagement, she should return to the Booths. Mrs Booth had actually made an appointment to take her to a physician on the following day, as she was in a very critical state of health. So in the morning I was obliged to send her back to Clapton by a faithful servant, going with them myself to the railway station. Though I was broken down with grief, she was unmoved. As a soldier of the Salvation Army, she had a duty to perform—she had performed it to the best of her ability; but having failed, she returned to her "General" disconcerted.

The Booths having thus failed in their object, now wished to get rid of my child. They sent her off to the railway station by a servant to go down to her married sister. But she would not go. I next heard of her from a friend as being alone in a lodging-house somewhere at the West End of London. However, she returned after a few days to the Booths, and was taken in, I suppose because they felt that in her state of health, insanity or death might be the consequence of further exposure to fatigue and harassment.

In consequence of hearing that the Booths had thus turned her out of their house, I immediately planned to find her a home in some cheerful pleasant Christian family, feeling that it was not only undesirable but impossible to have her now with me. I inserted advertisements in the London papers, and had more than fifty replies, mostly from clergymen. I selected one which presented a very favourable opening. It was in a beautiful Rectory House, twenty miles from London. I went down to see the clergyman and his wife. Never shall I forget the kindness and sympathy of those dear Christian people. It would have been a delightful home for my child, where she would have had refined and cultivated society, interesting work in the Sunday school, and visiting the poor, and every comfort which the house of a clergyman of wealth and high social position could have yielded. I wrote immediately to her, telling her of my arrangement, but alas she had already returned to the Booths, and under their influence there was no hope of her carrying out my wishes.

The following letter, written to Mrs Booth, will explain what I was endeavouring to do:—

"BEAUCHAMP ROAD, NORWOOD, S.E.
"*24th November* 1883.

"Mrs Booth,

"Madam,—I am ill. I have risen from my bed to write this letter, as it is so important I should have a reply. I have written two letters to my daughter this week requiring urgently a reply. She has written two most painful letters to me; one I received late last night, but leaving my questions entirely unnoticed. Some time since I heard that you and Mr Booth wished that my daughter's connection with you should cease; that you had sent her to the station to go to her sister's house, but that she instead of going there had gone to the house of some lady at the West End, whom she had met in Switzerland. I wrote to her urging her to come home to me, she declined. You refused at Little Amwell to use your influence to induce her to return to me. Under these painful circumstances of my daughter being virtually homeless, I set about the effort of seeking a home for her. I have been in correspondence with thirty clergymen on the subject. I have, after much consideration, selected the house of a clergyman of eminent position, both in the church and socially, in whose delightful house and beautiful parish I think she might be most happy, and be engaged in active usefulness in the Lord's service.

"I wrote to her to meet me, that I might take her to this clergyman's house to judge for herself. She takes no notice of my letters. He has twice come up to London to see me, and I have been down to his parish to see him and his wife, and I am so pleased with everything. But if my daughter is not happy there, I can easily find another home. I have the choice from thirty clergymen's houses. You told me that I was an old man, and that it was not fit a young girl should live in my dull house. These are all bright homes, with young people and active fathers and mothers.

"But I must have at once my child's decision. She ought to have gone down with me to-day to the clergyman of whom I have spoken. She and I were expected there yesterday or to-day. There must be no further delay. I must go with her on Monday or Tuesday, or she must write to me saying that she declines, and decides to continue with you and the Army. Then our course of action is determined. Our intercourse must cease, for I can bear these harassing harrowing letters no longer. I will allow her sufficient for all her personal expenses, to be paid monthly through my bankers or yours as arranged. She writes to me to pay to her £50 which I and her mother invested in the funds in our joint names for her when she reached twenty-one,

her sisters having the same amount. But I cannot give her this now, as it was not her mother's wish or intention that she should have it before twenty-one. My eldest daughter had hers when she was twenty-one, the second has not yet had hers, not being twenty-one. I have also £8 which Maud had placed in the Savings Bank. This she can have at once with interest. She says she is wanting winter clothes, and to go away for change of air. When she was last here, I arranged to take her off immediately to the sea-side, and I am willing to do so at once, but she must not go alone. There is no expense, there is no effort, there is no sacrifice I will not make for her, but it must be made on some certain course of action, some definite decision. All this miserable uncertainty, these bickerings, mis-statements, and heart-burnings are only destroying the health, the peace of mind, and the useful activities of both of us. Some decision must be come to, and then acted upon. I will abide by it. It is impossible to go on longer in this harassing line of conduct. I expect to hear from Maud decisively on Monday.—Believe me, yours faithfully,
"SAMUEL CHARLESWORTH."

I received no answer to this letter. Mrs Booth took no notice of it, but the following letter from Maud was written from the house at Clapton:—

"THE SALVATION ARMY, 114 CLAPTON COMMON,
November 24*th*, 1883.

"My Dear Father,—In my last letter I stated my decision never to give up the Army most plainly. I can say nothing more but repeat it, and add that this decision will never change. Still, as I have stated, I never wished to give you up as my father, and shall never do so, though, if necessary, I must accept your decision to give me up as your daughter for belonging to the Salvation Army, which I first joined with your consent. Your loving child, "MAUD E. CHARLESWORTH."

The following is my reply:—

"BEAUCHAMP ROAD, NORWOOD, S.E.
26th November 1883.

"Dear Maud,—It is wrong of you to say that you joined the Army with my consent. I have never given my consent directly or indirectly. I have simply left you to take your own course and choice, because I could not divert your will. I most deeply deplore your decision. But after having made such earnest appeals to you to return home to me, I must now regard the matter as settled, and leave you to your own undutiful, misguided course. I know not how you or those with whom you are associated can ever expect a blessing from on High to attend your union to the Army. You have by your conduct broken down my health, destroyed my home happiness, and thrown upon my declining years a shadow of the deepest sorrow and anxiety.

"I enclose you a cheque for £20, and will thank you to return me *the receipt signed by the first post to-morrow.*

"As to the power which I may exercise in disposing of my property, that will depend much upon your future course of action. Neither your dear Aunt Maria, nor your beloved mother, nor your dear grandpapa would ever for one moment have desired that any property derived through them should go to the Booth family or to the Salvation Army. Whatever I do and arrange, that must be avoided.

"My child, if we do not meet again on earth, remember I fully and freely forgive you all the pain, grief, and harassment you have caused me. I must lay much to the charge of your own wilful perverseness and undutifulness, but others are more to blame than you, for they could at any time have guided you into the right path of loving obedience and thoughtful submission.

"God will requite them for all the misery they have caused me. It is utterly impossible that true love to God and fidelity to the service of the Lord Jesus Christ can be the motive power or principles of action in persons who have acted as they have acted towards me. I am, dear Maud, your sorrowing, deeply wronged father, "SAMUEL CHARLESWORTH."

The following articles of marriage have to be subscribed by all who are married whilst belonging to the Army.

"ARTICLES of MARRIAGE which soldiers must agree to before the General will marry them.

"1. We solemnly declare that we do not seek this marriage simply to please ourselves, but that we believe it will enable us to better serve and please God, and serve the interests of The Salvation Army.

"2. We promise never to allow our marriage to lessen in any way our devotion to God or to The Army.

"3. We each severally promise that we will never try to prevent each other doing or giving anything that is in our power to do or to give to help The Army.

"4. We each severally promise to use all our influence with each other to promote constant and entire self-sacrifice for the Salvation of the world.

"5. We promise always to regard and arrange our home in every way as a Salvation Army Soldiers' (or Officers') quarters, and to train everyone in it to faithful service in The Salvation Army.

"6. We promise, whether together or apart, always to do our utmost as Soldiers of The Salvation Army, and never to allow it to be injured or hindered by anyone without doing our best to prevent or overcome such injury or hindrance.

"7. Should either of us cease to be an efficient Soldier, owing to sickness, death, or any other cause, we engage that the remaining one shall continue to the best of his or her ability to fulfil all these promises."

CHAPTER IX.

IN a former chapter I have stated that when I went to the house at Clapton to bring away my daughter, I was compelled, in consequence of the language addressed to me, to leave the sitting room and remain waiting at the hall door until she was ready to accompany me. Mrs Booth on that occasion asked me how I, as a professed minister of the Gospel, dared to take away my daughter from the service of Christ to which she had devoted herself. This and much more uttered in the same strain made me resolve never to enter that house again, the tone of which was so alien to the mind and spirit of the Lord Jesus Christ. But I must show how the influence of that family deteriorated the character of my poor child.

When she again, on her second return from Switzerland, without my consent went to the house, she wrote to one of my servants to bring her some articles of dress from home which she needed. I directed the servant to give them only to my daughter, and to insist upon seeing her, that I might know how she was and felt from her own lips. Before entering the house at Clapton, my servant on looking up at the window from the garden gate saw Maud in the front parlour sitting at a table with one of the children. On entering the house she requested to see my daughter. The servant brought back word from Mrs Booth that Miss Charlesworth was ill and could see no one. My faithful servant, true to my instructions, refused to give up the clothes, and insisted on seeing her. After some delay she was shewn upstairs to a room at the top of the house, where she found my daughter in bed; but she felt quite sure that at the time she had on her day dress. On another occasion, when I was ill, confined to my bed in Gloucestershire, a private letter from a friend informed me that Maud was ill at Clapton. I wrote immediately to my eldest daughter at Clapham to go and see her sister. On entering the house she was shewn into a little back parlour, and soon the servant brought down word that Maud would not see her sister. My daughter then wrote a line to her urgently entreating that, as she had been directed to come by me, Maud would see her. Again the servant returned, saying that Maud would not see her. My daughter, feeling sure that Mrs Booth was directing or influencing these messages, sent up word that she must see her sister, and on that occasion followed the servant upstairs. On entering the room Maud would hardly speak to her. I had a letter from my poor child afterwards, saying that if her sister was sent to her again, she would lock herself into her room and refuse to see her. I mention this to shew how demoralising was the influence thus exerted over a child who two years before had been one of the most loving, gentle, truthful, and devoted of children in her home. So soon as I was able to travel I returned home to Clapham. Whilst still confined through weakness to the sofa and hardly able to walk, a telegram came from Maud at Clapton saying that she wanted to see me, and would within half-an-hour from my receipt of the telegram meet me near Clapham Church. Though not equal to the effort I went out to see my poor child. As I anticipated, the interview was only to obtain my consent to her immediate marriage to the very son of whom I had been told most positively that he was engaged to another young lady of large fortune connected with the Army, on the strength of which statement I had refrained from making my daughter a ward of Chancery, and thus by the authority of the Court having her removed from the house of the Booths. I had never spoken to that son or heard from him by letter, and now that he was about to embark for Australia on the following Thursday they sought to force me to consent to their marriage. Heartrending as the interview with my poor infatuated child was, I felt that I could not give my sanction to a marriage under such circumstances. As a clergyman I could not endure the mockery of a Salvation Army marriage, in which the parties are married in the name of the Army and into the Army, and are bound by the most solemn previous pledge to let no marriage duties or engagements at all interfere with their Army service—in fact, binding themselves to obey in all things the commands of the "General," so that the husband might be sent off to India, the wife to America, and the children left in the charge of strangers. Moreover, this very attempt to force me to consent was all in breach of the engagements entered into with me, and the assurances made to me by Mr and Mrs Booth, and Miss Booth and my daughter.

The following rules shew the Army regulations on this subject :

" 11. What is the rule of The Army with regard to marriage ?

" 1. Head-quarters is *not* opposed to marriages which promise the continued *happiness* and *usefulness* of the officers.

" 2. Head-quarters *is* opposed to marriages projected in haste and repented of at leisure, which lead to poverty, stop usefulness, and terminate in misery.

" 3. Head-quarters advises every officer to make up his or her mind that God can make and keep them happy, holy, and useful, *unmarried*. When officers have come to this conclusion, they will then be able to wait until He makes known his will in the matter.

" 4. No marriages can take place without the *consent* of head-quarters.

" 12. What is the rule of The Army with regard to courting ?

" 1. Those who *flirt*, and are found out, which is usually the case, are sent home again.

"2. Those who are proved guilty of wilful *jilting* are dismissed in disgrace.

"3. None are allowed to do any courting during the first twelve months.

"4. If, at the end of that time, any engagements are formed, information to this effect must be forwarded in confidence to the General-in-Chief, who, if he approves, gives consent to such engagement."

My interview with my poor child was most harrowing; she left me in great anger without a word of adieu.

On the following day, Tuesday, Mr Ballington Booth came down to Clapham. Ill as I was it was a great effort to me to see him. For four hours, from one o'clock to five, I had the mental torture of an interview with him, his demand that I should assent to his marriage being grounded on the assertion that it was the dying wish of my wife—a statement which was, as I told him, a pure invention, utterly untrue, from whomsoever it emanated. When he left me I was thoroughly exhausted in mind and body. I had retired to rest when at ten o'clock the same evening he brought down my daughter nine miles, all the way from Clapton, in a cab to make a further attempt to force from me a consent. Another harrowing half hour resulted of course in my refusal, when they both declared that they would notwithstanding marry. I then told Mr Ballington Booth that unless he instantly retracted those words the following morning an application would be made to the Court of Chancery for an injunction to restrain him. That was the last time I have seen my poor child, now nearly a year. I have had sorrowful letters from her since reproaching me for my cruelty, and saying that it had caused her a serious illness, and was bringing her to the grave. However, notwithstanding, since that she has been attending more than two hundred meetings in all parts of the United Kingdom, in which she has given addresses as the Swiss heroine, recounting the persecutions she and her comrades had undergone in Switzerland. Some thousands of pounds have poured into the Army Exchequer at head-quarters as the practical result of these stirring appeals from English, Welsh, Scotch, and Irish sympathisers. The Army could not have had a more effective champion of their cause; with a winning address, a sweet face, and an enthusiasm which carries an audience with her. My child has gained sympathy and admiration, and large collections wherever she has gone. William Booth has had an able officer for what he calls his field work; he has sent a young inexperienced girl unprotected throughout England, Wales, Scotland, and Ireland to repeat the exaggerated tale of Swiss intolerance and religious persecution.

The following is a copy of a letter I wrote to Mr Booth after my interview with his son:—

CLAPHAM COMMON, S.W.,
3rd July 1884.

"Sir,—I have had this week two very painful interviews with my daughter, Maud Charlesworth, and with your son, Mr Ballington Booth, in which they have both very urgently pressed upon me the subject of my consenting at once to their marriage. That no mistake may arise as to what passed in these interviews, I beg to inform you that having regard to what I consider to be the true and best interests of my poor misguided child, I refused, without any reservation or qualification, to give my consent to her marriage. As she entirely disregards my counsels and wishes, in consequence of having given herself up to the Army for life, and placed herself under your roof and control, I would suggest to you that it may be well that she should be aware that if she does so marry, she forfeits thereby the provision made for her under her late grandfather's will.

"I add this, because your son, in his second interview with me, stated in her presence that notwithstanding my refusal to consent he would marry her. I am, sir, yours obediently, "SAMUEL CHARLESWORTH."

"The Rev. William Booth."

CHAPTER X.

I WOULD fain close this painful narrative without another word. To write it thus far has been the greatest effort, the most trying ordeal of a long life, but I should leave the history incomplete did I not refer to the objectionable nature of the Orders and Regulations of the Army, and of its Doctrines and Discipline.

The Rev. Charles Bullock, in his forcible "Reply to the Secret Book of the Salvation Army," and the Countess de Gasparin in her two admirable pamphlets of criticism and condemnation of the Army with reference to its operations in Switzerland, have each exposed the unscriptural and immoral tendency of these two books. I need not, therefore, say much with regard to them. The first book, Orders and Regulations, is a common unrefined imitation of the Orders of the Jesuit system, based on the Romish axiom that the end justifies the means, and claiming for the General Commander-in-Chief more absolute despotic authority over the officers and soldiers of the Army than ever Ignatius Loyola sought to enforce over the members of his order.

The book of Doctrines and Discipline virtually ignores the sacraments of the Christian religion, speaks of the Bible as a *dead book*, not containing the whole mind and will of God, needful for the guidance of man, and assigning to the teaching and sayings of the authorised Army officers an equality in authority with the Holy Scriptures. It teaches, moreover, that all who truly join the Army and act in conformity with its doctrine and discipline are without sin. It holds all other denominations of Christians as in error and alien from God, and claims for the Army such an infallibility as the most arrogant of popes and the most dogmatic decrees of councils never asserted to be due to the Church of Rome.

It is because I so object to the principles and teaching of these two books that, as a Christian father and a clergyman of the Church of England, I have opposed the efforts of Mr Booth and his family to allure away my daughter from her home, and to alienate her from me and her family, and other relatives and the church of her youth. As her father, upon me devolves the responsibility of her religious and moral training, and by what right do Mr and Mrs Booth step in between me and my child, to deprive me of that control which both the law of God and the law of man ordain that I should possess and exercise. I know not that I should ever have felt it obligatory upon me to have said or written a word upon the subject of the Army had not my daughter been thus associated with it, for I should probably have continued as ignorant of its principles and practice as the majority of Christians are; but having suffered so greatly in health of body and of mind, through the distress and anxiety I have been occasioned in the breaking up of the peace and happiness of my home, and in the hinderance to my ministerial work, I claim a right to denounce that system which has caused such grievous injury and cruel wrong to me and my family. The Army system is based on the principle that all rights, claims, and duties of social life and church membership in every form must yield to its sweeping demands and paramount importance.

I ask by what right do Mrs Booth and her daughters dare to counsel children to leave their homes and occupations in opposition to the wishes and commands of their parents and employers; and by what right or authority, divine or human, has Mr Booth presumed to institute a religious system in which he arrogates to himself as Commander and General-in-Chief, deputed by and in the place of God, the most absolute power of controlling and directing not only adult members of his Army system, but young persons under age who have left their parents, their homes or employments at his instigation?

Why also does he assume to himself the power to commission his subordinates to bear honourable titles of distinction which can only be rightly obtained by years of hard and dangerous service, and through the possession of able talents and industrious study and training? Even the captains of trading vessels and of mines need long experience and training, and must give evidence of ability in order to attain the recognised position of captains.

If Mr Booth chooses to make young girls vain and ridiculous by dubbing them Marechales, Majors, Captains, Lieutenants, Aidés-de-Camp, &c., the weakness and folly of such an absurd practice deprive it of harm. But when he scatters over the United Kingdom and the World at large, bearded and moustached young men dressed in uniform, with military and naval titles, allowing them in travelling about and in hotels to be so addressed and spoken to among strangers ignorant of the deception, I say that such conduct is not only religiously a fraud, but socially and nationally a grievous wrong. What warrant has he for it in Scripture? There is only one Captain mentioned there, the Captain of our salvation, who was made perfect through suffering. Even in the Jesuit order from which he copies so largely, there were no such titles assigned or assumed. The title of General adopted by the head was only a substitute for our word chief or principal, and was never used as a conventional appellation or mode of ordinary address.

I once read in the *War Cry* an order from headquarters, that Mrs Booth should be addressed as Mrs General Booth, and I have seen her so described in large letters on street placards in Limehouse.

Even my daughter in my presence in that painful interview to which I have alluded, addressed Mr Booth's son as Colonel. This assumption of titles, only belonging to men of position, has made some of the ignorant men of the Army so conceited and arrogant that it is painful to have dealings with them. I knew one, a poor labouring man, who had been so long called Captain, that he would have felt quite insulted if the title had been omitted, and his blustering authoritative manner was almost equal to his General's bearing.

I have one more explanation to make. The Book of Orders and Regulations is published now, and can only be obtained as a little book of one part, but it was written, if not published, as a large book of six parts. Since the publication of the Countess de Gasparin's strictures on this first part, I suppose it has been deemed expedient or prudent to suppress the other five parts. It has even been asserted that the other five parts never existed, were never written. The Countess in her unanswerable pamphlet, "A Simple Request to Mr Booth," has clearly proved the moral impossibility that the first part could have been written as it now stands without the writer having before him the other five parts. At all events the question results itself thus: either the statement that the other five parts never existed is untrue, or else fifty-three references in the first part are positively false and misleading, such as the following :—

Page 1. "The objects for which this Army exists are fully described and dwelt upon in part 5 of this book, which must be carefully studied by everyone who is anxious to excel in usefulness."

Page 9. "Let one of the six parts, or by preference as variety makes the study easier, one chapter out of each, be fixed upon for attention each day—Monday the first chapter of each part (and so on every day)."

Then follow numerous directions to read carefully, &c., the parts, the chapter, and the section of the other five parts for further particulars, full information, instructions, and explanation, &c., of part 1.

Page 8. "It is said the size of this book may cause some to fear lest they may never be able to grasp, much less to carry out all its contents."

Part I is a little book, about 4 inches square and a quarter of an inch thick.

When I wrote to the *Times*, I was ignorant of the difference between Orders and Regulations which I had read, and Doctrines and Discipline which I had only momentarily glanced at by taking it up accidentally, and, being the same size and colour, assuming it to be the same book as the other. Therefore I referred to the suppressed and concealed book as a secret book without definitely describing it, but Mr Booth knew what I meant. However, he chose to affix the character of secret book to the book of Doctrines and Discipline, as though I had referred to that, and was very facetious about it at one of the great meetings at Exeter Hall, placarding the hall with notices that the secret book could be purchased by any one for 6d., and so referring to it as the secret book in the addenda of an altered edition, thus blinding the public as to the really suppressed or withheld book by turning attention from the five unobtainable parts of Orders and Regulations, and fixing it upon the entirely separate and different book of Doctrines and Discipline, which was complete in itself.

What shall I say with regard to the Army as a whole? What I have said or written a hundred times and more —that it has done a wonderful work in the reformation of the immoral, the vicious, the abandoned. Then why so condemn it? I do not condemn it in its noble work by the devoted, self-sacrificing, earnest, enthusiastic young people, who, like my daughter, have been led, out of love to Christ and to souls, to join in it and work for it. But I do condemn it, as I have to my sorrow and my loss seen its principles carried out into practice by the Booth family, by inducing the young to renounce and ignore their home-duties and social obligations. The Booths have abused me for seeking to keep back my daughter from the Lord's service. Yet she had long been my loving helper in my parochial schools, and other useful Christian work. But with the Booths nothing is in the Lord's service if not in the Army service, nothing is the Lord's work outside the Army barracks or operations. Had my child wished to go as a missionary worker to India, Africa, China, or elsewhere, gladly would I have given her up to any church, society, or well-ordered Christian mission. But when the Booths by their system alienated and separated my child from me and her home at the age of sixteen, and fostered in her an attachment to a man, who, without my knowledge, constituted himself her father confessor and spiritual adviser, and when, in answer to my earnest appeals and remonstrances, they treated me with coarse rudeness, set me at defiance, and counselled my child to do the same, and when they schemed to effect her marriage, in breach of solemn promises made to me, then I thought and said, surely these people are not the followers or servants of the Lord Jesus Christ; and I agreed with Lord Shaftesbury, Dean Close, and other eminent philanthropists and ministers, who regarded such conduct as more Satanic than Christ-like.

I remembered what St Paul had written of certain in the Church at Corinth who were "false apostles, deceitful workers, transforming themselves into the apostles of Christ, and no marvel, for Satan himself is transformed into an angel of light. Therefore it is not a great thing if his ministers also be transformed as the ministers of righteousness, whose end shall be according to their works." I recalled also what the same Apostle wrote to Timothy, warning him "that in the last days perilous times should come, for men should be lovers of their own selves, covetous, boasters, proud, blasphemers, disobedient to parents, unthankful, unholy, without natural affection, truce breakers, false accusers, fierce, despisers of those that are good, traitors, heady, high minded, having a form of godliness but denying the power thereof, from such turn away."

This is what General Booth taught my child when she placed herself under his direction and counsel.

Orders and Regulations, page 2. "God works by one person upon another. This implies that He (God) can only do His utmost *by persons who are in the most perfect and continual subjection to those whom he has chosen to lead them.*"

Page 4. "We must write the military principles in every mind and heart."

Page 18. "But every one should be particularly on their guard against accepting as a Divine impulse any impressions which go against the plain principles of the service."

Page 56. "Moreover it is often by keeping a salvation meeting going for a long time that conviction reaches that intense and agonising pitch which produces the best results."

Page 60. "But a field-officer on taking command must always be firm in believing and declaring his Divine errand to the people, and therefore satisfied of his own value to them as a light. A man who relies for congregations and success upon the speaking of others is not fit for the position.

"The field-officer is not obliged to follow any rule of other preachers, and need take no Scripture text. He must not keep to any one subject. He is at liberty to follow the guidance of the Holy Ghost, *and to give to the people as from God whatever he feels bound to tell them.*

"But a field-officer is bound to act as God's ambassador to the town to which he goes."

Doctrines and Discipline, page 3. "But was not the Holy Ghost given to the Apostles on the day of Pentecost?

"Yes, the Spirit was given them in a special measure then, and through them to the world generally. The day of Pentecost was to the Apostles and early disciples what many all-nights or special meetings are to the Salvation Army people now-a-days—a day of special endowment for the work before them. But He, the Holy Spirit, had been working on mankind from the beginning."

Page 39. "How does the Holy Spirit seek to bring about the submission and salvation of men?

"By raising up men and women to fight for God. By qualifying them with wisdom, love, and zeal; by giving them thoughts and messages direct from Himself, and by sustaining and comforting them in the conflict."

When it is remembered from what and from whom these Salvation Army teachers are taken, from the most vicious, depraved, and uneducated, apply the foregoing rules to them, and tremble for the consequences.

CHAPTER XI.

HAD Mr and Mrs Booth raised themselves from a position of poverty and obscurity to one of wealth and eminence by industry, thrift, and ability in trade or literature, as many successful merchants, manufacturers, and professional men during the present century have risen, from a low estate to one of great usefulness and high rank, I should have been the last person, I hope, to have recalled or commented upon their early antecedents of indigence and meanness; but when they have made a profession of religion the stepping-stone from a very low and poor condition to one of great responsibility, publicity, and influence, they have laid themselves and their schemes and doings open to investigation and criticism by all who are injuriously and prejudicially affected by their conduct. And surely no one has a greater right to discuss their character and conduct than a father who has suffered so cruelly and wrongfully by the system of proselytism they have originated and prosecuted, that father being an aged clergyman. More especially is this the case as my young daughter, allured and alienated from me and her home, her relatives and the Church of her youth, was at the early age of sixteen years, when a girl at school, drawn into an attachment to one of the sons, a man seven or eight years her senior, of whom I knew nothing, and whose only opportunity of thus gaining her affections was in his interviews with her at professedly religious meetings. Since Mr Booth established his system, so strangely called the Salvation Army, he has raised and possessed money and property to the extent of more than two millions in value, three-fourths of which have been drawn from the poor, and of this money and property he has constituted himself the sole receiver, treasurer, comptroller, and spender. Inasmuch as my daughter is a minor of the age of nineteen years, and supported by me, I am legally entitled to call upon Mr Booth for an account of the large sums of money she has, at a great risk to health, earned for him. Not that I would for one moment claim to receive one shilling of such money, but I can demand of him to know how he has appropriated and expended it. Had Mr Booth employed the vast sums that he has raised in philanthropical and benevolent works, such as providing for destitute children, as many evangelistic workers for the Lord have done during the last forty years, I would be silent on this painful subject; but when I know that thousands upon thousands have been spent in hotel expenses, railway journies, four-horse coaches, in processions, in telegrams, banners, musical instruments, and in many similar ways, in which no other collectors of charitable funds would ever think of appropriating money entrusted to them, I feel that I am justified in contrasting his antecedents of poverty and obscurity with his present position of lavish expenditure and ostentatious display, and asking by what means, from what sources, the son of the joiner at Nottingham, brought up for many years as a pawnbroker's assistant, and living in humble lodgings at Brixton, and marrying the daughter of lowly parents residing in Russell Street, Brixton, has been enabled to live in the house on Clapton Common and to provide for all the numerous expenses which are entailed by his elevated position of General and Commander-in-Chief of his Army, with so numerous a retinue of Field, Staff Officers, Aides-de-Camp, Marèchals, Colonels, Majors, Captains, Lieutenants, Adjutants, and Cadets, with all their uniforms, insignia of rank, banners, brass bands, drums, and other accoutrements of war. Will he dare to refer to Him, who was, when on earth, always the meek and lowly One, the Man of Sorrows, the Son of poverty, who had not where to lay His head, and of whom it was said, He shall not strive nor cry, neither shall any man hear His voice in the streets? or will he dare to point to those humble, earnest, simple-minded Galilean fishermen and peasants, as his models, his exemplars? The Lord once rode on a borrowed colt in a triumphal procession, but it was on His way to the cross. What mockery! what travesty of our holy religion is a system so opposed to all that the Scriptures enjoin in the followers of Jesus, so in accord with all that Christ and His apostles would condemn. Verily the General and Commander-in-chief and his officers of this pseudo Army in sounding a trumpet before them in the barracks and in the streets, that they may have glory of men, have their reward of notoriety; his followers break the rest of the holy Sabbath, disturb quiet and peaceful towns and villages, stir up opposition and engender strife, draw away children from their Sunday schools, is all this Christ-like? It may get the Army officers before the magistrates, into prison, and so drag them into public notice in the newspapers, but it was not so that Saints Peter, John, James, and Paul became inmates of dungeons and sufferers by stripes. Let the general and his officers beware, lest in thus courting and provoking the enforcement of just legal restraint unfairly stigmatised as persecution, they receive the reward of the hypocrites of old, of whom Christ said, "For they love to pray standing in the corners of the streets, that they may be seen of men."

How much does all that I have said on this painful subject apply to the mournful proceedings in Switzerland? There is no European country which the Army could have invaded where the habits, customs, and feelings of the people could have been more opposed and outraged by Army practices than in Switzerland. For a young girl to appear on a public platform, to address the audience, or for one not affianced to travel about and consort with young unmarried men, would at once stamp such offenders against the rules of Swiss propriety and decorum, as persons utterly unworthy of esteem. Even at hotels they refused to receive the Salvationists, and I believe that the visits of Miss Booth to my hotel would have caused my being sent away had they been continued. They made me feel most uncomfortable, because I knew how this breach of Swiss etiquette had been a reproach upon the Army.

What is the consequence in Switzerland and also in France of the Army's proceedings; that the work of God's true servants, the real earnest consistent Christian evangelists, has been greatly impeded and marred. The French and Swiss people, unaware how little these extravagances and improprieties have countenance in England, regard the religion of the Salvationists as a sample of English protestantism.

And so throughout the world, Christian and heathen, the absurdities and inconsistencies of the Army destroy the simplicity and purity, and mar the beauty of the Gospel of our Lord and Saviour Jesus Christ. The *War Cry* may utter its boasts of victory; may recount how thousands of red-hot sinners have gone up to the penitent form, the mercy-seat, the altar, and plunged into the blood fountain, and come out saved and sanctified in red jerseys, through the excursion trains of the Holy Ghost from heaven (I am quoting well-known phrases from the *War Cry*), but whether those thus said to be converted have been raised from the death of sin unto the life of righteousness, God alone knows. That drunkards and other immoral, vicious, and criminal men have been reclaimed under the influence of the earnest self-denying loving labours of many of the young teachers I am sure, and so far the work has been a noble and blessed one; but sobriety is not of necessity sanctification, nor is morality salvation. I know not how the Lord of life and glory can use as His instrumentality in building up His Church on earth a system which in its doctrines and practice is so opposed to His teaching and to the mind and will of God as revealed in the Bible.

General Booth at every meeting, while deploring the

deficiency of the funds, boasts of the great increase of his forces. He revels in figures. Addition and multiplication as applied to his stations, officers, corps, members, and periodicals are his favourite rules in arithmetic. But increase in members is no evidence of purity in doctrine or stability in the faith.

In closing my mournful history, I would say to the relatives and dear friends for whose perusal alone it is intended, do not judge of my conduct as a father and a Christian minister from what is said on platforms or written in newspapers, or even stated in private conversations by my daughter and her associates. For three years I have had a most difficult task to perform, first striving to retain my daughter in her home and in love and obedience to me. I failed utterly because of the influence brought to bear in opposition or counteraction. Then I appealed to the Booths, and sought to move them by all the arguments and entreaties a father could use. I might as well have appealed to a nether mill stone or to the Niagara cataract. I then sought to fence my child around by exacting promises and assurances as conditions to my leaving her to her own course and will. They were all snapped asunder as tow made only to be broken. I have not given a detail of one-tenth of what I have undergone and suffered, as the record of one thousand letters and other documents would prove, but at present I must rest my case on this mere glimpse of what has passed. I can only say from this scant record, learn a part of my suffering and sorrow, and judge the character of the whole. God knows how I loved that child and sought to rescue her from what I felt to be impending evil, and He knows also how I have been thwarted and rendered hopeless and helpless. In His hands I am willing to leave the issue. To His judgment I can appeal in confidence. The future shall decide the terrible question between me and William Booth and his family—not between me and my child and the Salvation Army. I throw the whole burden of responsibility and retribution upon William Booth, his wife, and children.

www.ingramcontent.com/pod-product-compliance
Lightning Source LLC
LaVergne TN
LVHW061218060426
835508LV00014B/1353